THE SOCIAL POLICY AND AGEING RESEARCH CENTRE

The Social Policy and Ageing Research Centre (SPARC) in Trinity College Dublin provides fresh, rigorous thinking on social policy as it relates to the ageing population in Ireland and in the global context. The centre draws on policy and practice in Ireland and other countries to generate insights into ways in which social policies can better serve older people.

No Place Like Home

Domiciliary Care Services for
Older People in Ireland

Virpi Timonen, Martha Doyle *and* David Prendergast
Social Policy and Ageing Research Centre
Trinity College Dublin

The Liffey Press

Published by
The Liffey Press
Ashbrook House, 10 Main Street
Raheny, Dublin 5, Ireland
www.theliffeypress.com

A catalogue record of this book is
available from the British Library.

ISBN 978-1-905785-01-8

Printed in Ireland by ColourBooks Ltd.

CONTENTS

Acknowledgements vii

Preface.. ix

1. Introduction and Background 1
Virpi Timonen

2. Research Methods 15
Virpi Timonen and David Prendergast

3. The Historical and Systemic Context............................... 31
Virpi Timonen and Martha Doyle

4. The State: Role in the Financing and Provision of Home Care ... 47
David Prendergast

5. The Non-Profit Sector: Role in the Provision of Home Care 81
David Prendergast

6. The Market: Role in the Provision of Home Care..................... 115
Martha Doyle

7. Comparison of the Private, Public and Non-profit Sectors 177
Virpi Timonen and Martha Doyle

8. Evolving Care Policies and Future Directions 201
Virpi Timonen and Martha Doyle

9. Conclusion.. 219
Virpi Timonen

Bibliography.. 229

ACKNOWLEDGEMENTS

We wish to thank the following individuals who assisted our work in various ways. As always, the authors alone, and none of the individuals named below, are responsible for the contents of this book:

Colette Garry, Research Executive Officer in the Social Policy and Ageing Research Centre, TCD, for her very competent and thorough copy-editing, formatting and assistance with referencing this book.

Dr Eoin O'Sullivan, School of Social Work and Social Policy, TCD, for loan of documents and advice regarding sources used in Chapter 3.

Atlantic Philanthropies, for supporting the Ageing Research Centre.

Janet Convery (HSE), Regina Buckley (HSE), Gerry Dolan (IMPACT) and Matt Merrigan (SIPTU) for offering advice at the early stages of our work.

Louise Halloran, for short-term research assistance.

Professor James Wickham and the Employment Research Centre, TCD for hosting a seminar where some of the preliminary results of this project were first discussed.

Professor Robbie Gilligan, School of Social Work and Social Policy, TCD, for words of advice and encouragement.

Members of the Advisory Board of the Ageing Research Centre, for their advice and support.

All the individuals who generously gave their time to be interviewed and to supply us with documentary materials. This research would not have been possible without their co-operation.

Note on Authorship

First and subsequent drafts of Chapters 1, 2, 3, 7, 8 and 9 were written by Virpi Timonen, reflecting the fact that she first drew up the outline of this study and decided to pursue it. Martha Doyle edited Chapters 1, 2, 3, 7, 8 and 9, and added substantially to Chapters 3, 7 and 8. Inputs by David Prendergast were incorporated into Chapter 2. Chapters 4 and 5 were written by David Prendergast, with structural and editorial advice and modifications by Martha Doyle and Virpi Timonen. Chapter 6 has been written by Martha Doyle, with advice and editing by Virpi Timonen.

The coherence of the book as a whole has been ensured by Virpi Timonen and Martha Doyle, and copy-editing, including some valuable stylistics and structural advice, was carried out by Colette Garry.

PREFACE

This book is the first major output of the Social Policy and Ageing Research Centre at Trinity College Dublin.[1] The Centre was established in 2005 with the view to producing and disseminating policy-relevant research in the area of ageing. The Centre is also a constituent part of the Trinity Consortium on Ageing,[2] an umbrella body that fosters research and teaching in the area of ageing.

The domiciliary (in-home) care for older people was selected as the initial flagship project because it represents a policy area of growing concern both in the Irish and international contexts. While much rhetorical emphasis is placed on the importance of enabling older people with care needs to remain living in their own homes (not in the least due to the increasing perception that many older people are in inappropriate institutional care settings in hospitals and nursing homes), the absence of baseline data and lack of a clear understanding of policy structures constitute significant obstacles to achieving this aim.

This study, conducted in August 2005-April 2006, involved interviewing 125 informants who are closely involved in planning, financing and delivering home care to older persons across Dublin. It represents the first systematic attempt in the Irish context to map out the respective roles and characteristics of the public, private and non-profit sector organisations involved in financing and delivering home care to older people.

---

[1] www.tcd.ie/Social_Studies/sparc/index.php

[2] www.tcd.ie/research/ageingconsortium

The book maps out the considerable shifts in the organisation and delivery of domiciliary care services for older persons over the last 10 years. A historical account is given of the shift from policy emphasis on institutional to domiciliary care. The increasing complexity of the "care mix" that has resulted from changes in the non-profit (formerly voluntary) sector and the emergence of the private sector care agencies, and their relationship to the State as purchaser of care services are analysed.

While the book is highly policy-relevant and includes a number of recommendations for changes in policy and practices, it also makes a major contribution to theory-building and historical analysis in the area of social care. As a result, the book is of interest to academic, policy and practitioner audiences, as well as postgraduate and undergraduate students, in the areas of social policy, politics, history of care services (the role of the voluntary sector in particular), sociology and social work. We also expect the book to be of interest to international readers, as it contains analysis that is of relevance for comparative research and theory-building in the area of social care. The most recent analysis of domiciliary care for older persons in Ireland was published in 1994;[3] our book fills a vacuum in an area that has changed rapidly and remained under-researched until now.

---

[3] Lundström, Francesca and Kieran McKeown (1994) *Home Help Services for Elderly People in Ireland*, Dublin: National Council for the Elderly.

Chapter 1

INTRODUCTION

Virpi Timonen

It is rarely acknowledged that most older persons are not in need of any care services and are able to live fully independently, often providing care to other younger or older relatives and friends such as grandchildren, spouse and neighbours. However, for those older persons who are in need of care, the availability, quality and cost of that care are obviously of paramount importance.

Ireland, alongside most other societies, is witnessing many extensive changes that arise from and impact upon its ageing population. Population ageing, in conjunction with other economic and social phenomena (such as declining family size and increased labour market participation among women), generates many new policy-related questions and challenges, and nowhere are these questions more acute and pressing than in the area of care.

The term "care" is multifaceted, as it relates to both health (medical/paramedical) and social care. The term social care is used to denote assistance with activities of daily living (ADL), i.e. personal care (washing, dressing, grooming etc.) or with instrumental activities of daily living (IADL), i.e. domestic work (cleaning, cooking, running errands etc.). Health and social care are naturally interlinked, although policies and institutions are not always able to ensure that these two types of care are provided in tandem or interchangeably. For instance, an older person may need to stay in hospital for a period when undergoing an operation or recuperating from a serious illness. Upon their recovery, a combination of medical and social services may be required to enable the older person to return to the home environment.

Both medical and social care is received in many different settings, and is carried out by a variety of carers ranging from medical professionals to family or informal carers. Figure 1.1 below sets out the basic structure of the complex social care mix that exists in Ireland. A basic distinction is made here between informal and formal care: informal care (on the left-hand side of the diagram) is often referred to as family care, denoting the fact that it is delivered by family members, neighbours or friends, in the recipient's or carer's home, usually without any financial recompense. Formal care, on the other hand, can be provided either in the community (in the home or in a public community setting such as a day care centre) or in an institution. As Figure 1.1 below illustrates, the actors involved in the provision of formal care can be drawn from the public (State), private (for-profit) or non-profit sectors.

The provision of formal social care in the home is most frequently called domiciliary care. This book focuses on the domiciliary care for older people in Ireland (Dublin), provided by the mix of public, private and non-profit actors. As policymakers in Ireland have put heavy (rhetorical) emphasis on "care in the home" (as opposed to institutional care) and as this is also the preferred setting for most people receiving care, it is important to gain a deeper understanding of the service providers who deliver this care in the home; the kind of assistance they provide; how they perceive their work; and how they relate to the older people they work with. This book is rooted in the belief that a deeper understanding of formal in-home care services is central both to the promotion of individual well-being in old age and to successful policy-making in ageing societies.

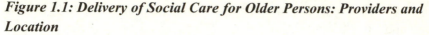

Figure 1.1: Delivery of Social Care for Older Persons: Providers and Location

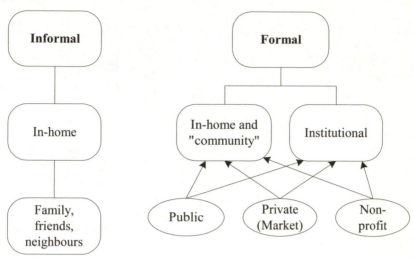

The financing of social care for older persons is no less complex than its provision: while the provider and financer are often indistinguishable (for instance, in the case of informal care the provider and de facto financer is often a family member), these roles are increasingly bifurcated. Figure 1.2 maps out the possible sources of financing for the social care of older persons. As can be seen on the left-hand side of the diagram, informal, family-provided care can be financed by the family exclusively, or by some combination of the family absorbing some of the (opportunity) costs, and the State partially subsidising the costs via, for instance, a carer's allowance or a cash-for-care benefit. The Irish version of cash-for-care (the newly-established home care packages) does not permit the channelling of this subsidy to family carers; only different kinds of formal providers can be used. However, in several other countries (e.g. the Netherlands, the UK and Austria) the cash-for-care benefit can be channelled to a family carer or a formal provider (for a comparative analysis of this international trend towards cash-for-care programmes, see Timonen, Convery and Cahill, 2006). With regard to formal care, the purchasers of this can be individuals or families (private) or the State (public) via a number of different universal or means-tested payments, towards all or part of the costs of care. These payments in turn can be tax- or social insurance-financed (for more detailed comparative analyses of financing long-term care of older people, see Timonen 2005 and 2006).

Figure 1.2: Financing Social Care for Older Persons

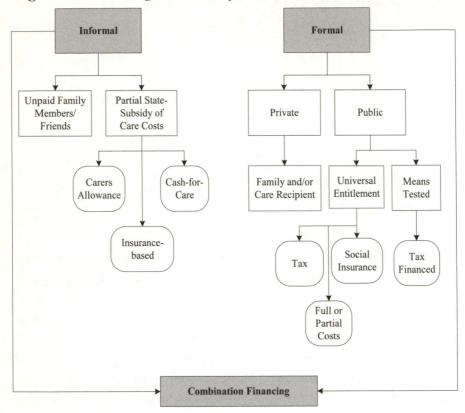

Background and Context of Research

A number of developments are widely intepreted as threatening the ability of the Irish care regime to provide the older population with the care and support that it needs. Firstly, the number of older persons is growing, and the growth is particularly fast in the 80+ category. Secondly, the number of older people living alone in Ireland is projected to increase dramatically in the next two decades with a doubling of the numbers between 2002 and 2021 for both males and females (Connell and Pringle, 2004). Thirdly, the rapid increase in women's labour market participation is often argued to severely restrict the supply of informal care. The question of shifts away from family and towards formal services is a much broader one than the one we are striving to answer here, and would require information on family inputs over time (which we do not have at present).

Lack of public (long-term care) beds, pressure on acute hospitals and the high costs and variable quality of institutional care have led to an increased focus on domiciliary care. Considerable consensus exists over the principle of enabling older persons to remain living in their own homes for as long as possible. However, explication of what exactly is meant by this is not generally provided, and the logic of the argument varies between economists, policy analysts and social workers. The thesis is often advanced that a large proportion of older persons in institutional care could in fact live in their own homes if provided with the right combination of services and modifications in their accommodation, and that the transitions from hospital or other medicalised care settings into a community care setting should be accelerated, both in the interest of the care recipient and in the interest of public finances. Yet very little is known of the transitions between these two care settings, of the preferences of individuals in different situations and of the kind of services and technologies that could accelerate and promote this transition. Comprehensive financial data which would provide comparisons of the costs of institutional care vis-à-vis home care for persons at different dependency levels and with different levels of informal care support is currently lacking in Ireland (although Hughes, Williams and Blackwell, 2004 contains a good preliminary comparison of the costs). Nonetheless, it is safe to say that there is a severe undersupply of domiciliary care services for older people in Ireland, a fact that is reflected both in the heavy strain that many informal carers operate under, and by the presence in institutional care settings of many individuals whose dependency level is defined as low.

Despite the fact that domiciliary care has received increased attention in policy-making in Ireland during recent years, we know surprisingly little about a number of salient aspects of "ageing in place". The list of gaps in our knowledge is extensive, and relates to all four core aspects of social services delivery that are included in Figure 1.3 below. Chapters 4, 5 and 6 of this book focus on the delivery and financing of in-home care by the public, non-profit and private sectors respectively, whilst Chapters 7, 8 and 9 venture into the areas of regulation and consumer power as part of a broader policy analysis.

Figure 1.3: Variables Influencing Social Service Delivery

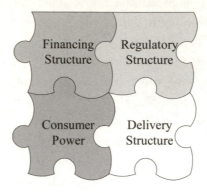

Source: Adapted from Alber (1995)

Table 1.1 below outlines the major knowledge gaps in the demand for and the delivery and financing structure of home care services. It was not possible to address the question concerning the demand for domiciliary care within the scope of this study.[1] However, the knowledge gaps relating to the provision and financing of domiciliary care services are extensively explored in this book.

Table 1.1: Knowledge Gaps in the Domiciliary Care Field

Demand Side	Supply Side	
Who needs care in the home?	*Who provides care in the home?*	*Who finances care in the home?*
Need to assess extent of difficulties with ADL and IADL. Explore the views and experiences of domiciliary care users.	Family/individuals State Voluntary sector Private sector	Family/individuals State (Voluntary sector)

---

[1] We do not know the extent of the need for care among the older community-dwelling population in Ireland. In the absence of a nationally representative study that is able to group older persons into a set of meaningful categories expressing the extent of their in/dependence, it is not possible to estimate the potential demand for care. It is expected that TILDA, the first Irish Longitudinal Study on Ageing, with its representative sample of ca. 10,000 older adults, will fill this gap in knowledge when its first wave is carried out in 2007/08.

Studies of the supply side of home care that have been conducted to date in Ireland have been very valuable, but limited to a particular segment of the care services sector. The most recent comprehensive overview of domiciliary care services for older people in Ireland was published in 1994 (Lundstrom and McKeown, 1994). While reference was made in this study to the emerging direct public provision of home care (through the newly-established role of home care attendants), the research focused almost exclusively on the role of the non-profit sector in the provision of domiciliary care ("home help"). This bias towards measuring the level of activity in the non-profit sector persists to this day in official government statistics. For instance, data on the number of hours of home help provided is generated on an annual basis. However, these annual statistics provide a very limited and partial insight into the extent of service provision in Ireland because firstly, the number of people who receive this service is not recorded and secondly, "home help" (the care typically delivered via these non-profits organisations) is only one type of formal care service that an older person may receive in their own home. Furthermore the hours of home help provided are not disaggregated by the number of recipients. This means that it is not possible to know whether a large number of hours are provided to a small group of clients or conversely a small number of hours are provided to a large number of people. Table 1.2 below lists the total number of hours provided in 2003 and 2004 and divides this by the number of persons aged 70 and over in Ireland. Naturally, the majority of these do not receive home help but in the absence of other information, this division indicates that if the hours were evenly distributed, the average person aged 70 or over in Ireland would have received some 30 hours of home help per annum in 2003 and 2004.

Table 1.2: Hours of Home Help Provided in Ireland, 2003 and 2004

Year	Hours of Home Help	Hours per 70+ Person
2003	8,828,899	29.0
2004	8,963,383	28.8

Source: Department of Health and Children, 2005.

Moreover, while the Department of Health and Children provides information on the total expenditure per annum on home help services, it is not possible to estimate the expenditure per recipient. However, using the crude methods applied above, the expenditure per 70+ person in Ireland did increase significantly between 2000 and 2001, but has remained largely static since then (see Table 1.3 below). As the figures are not adjusted to take inflation and salary increases[2] into account, in real terms expenditure per person may have declined.

Table 1.3: Home Help Budget per Capita for 70+ Population, per Annum (€ million)

Year	Total € Million	€ Per 70+ Person
2000	51.7	175
2001	102.3	343
2002	105.1	348
2003	111.5	364
2004	126.6	406

Source: Department of Health and Children, 2005.

How does the provision of domiciliary care in Ireland compare with that of other countries? The proportion of the older (65+) population in receipt of formal home care services varies considerably between countries, as can be seen from Table 1.4 below. Note, however, that this table, as is the case for most comparative datasets, only relates to home care services that are publicly provided or financed from the public purse. For example, around 20 per cent of Norwegian and British older people are in receipt of state-funded domiciliary care, in contrast with only 5 per cent of older Irish people. While this does mean that fewer people in Ireland are in receipt of formal care services sponsored or provided by the state, it does not necessarily mean that the overall proportion of older

---

[2] According to information received from the Department of Health and Children in March 2005, the considerable increase between 2000 and 2001 is due to the introduction of the minimum wage in April 2000. Prior to this date, many home help workers had been receiving payments substantially below the minimum wage, whereas after this date, they were eligible to receive the minimum wage, or higher.

persons in receipt of some level of care in their own home is considerably lower. The lower coverage of formal services is doubtlessly compensated for by informal (family) care, although in the absence of comprehensive data we cannot be sure of the precise extent of this compensation. Nonetheless, the overall picture that emerges from this comparative data is the relatively low level of public provision in the area of home care for older persons in Ireland.

Table 1.4: Percentage of 65+ Population Receiving Home Care Services, Selected Countries, Most Recent Year for which Data is Available

Country	Per Cent of 65+ in Receipt of Home Help
Australia	14.7
Austria	14.8
Germany	7.1
Ireland	ca. 5
Japan	5.5
Netherlands	12.3
Norway	18.0
Sweden	9.1
UK	20.3
US	2.8

Source: OECD, 2005

As was stated above, the statistical information currently available in Ireland is indicative only of the level of public provision and financing of home care services, and even in this area they are insufficient and vague.

Over the last decade private for-profit care agencies have emerged and appear to be playing an increasingly significant role in the overall care mix in Ireland. As a result, the present methods of data collection and presentation are inadequate and even misleading. No reference was made to private care agencies in the 1994 report by Lundstrom and McKeown (1994), presumably because only one or two private care agencies were in existence before the mid-1990s. The emergence, expansion and proliferation of the private domiciliary care sector for community-dwelling older persons in Ireland is a major development that has extensive policy-making implications. Chapter 6 of this book represents the first systematic attempt in the Irish context to analyse the key features of the private sector as a provider of home care services for older persons.

In addition to the emergence and expansion of the private care sector, many significant changes have taken place in the public and non-profit sectors. The most significant development in recent years with respect to the non-profit sector has been the improvement in the employment terms and conditions of workers in this sector. In 2000, the rights and working conditions of home helps began to be regulated and increasing numbers are now becoming unionised with SIPTU. Most home help organisers (managers) are unionised in Impact.

The pay and benefits of home helps have improved significantly, but many issues, particularly the need for training and "upskilling", remain to be addressed.

At the time of publication of the 1994 report, home care attendants were a new phenomenon in Ireland. The home care attendant service was created as part of the community nursing service: this group of workers has subsequently been renamed "health care assistants". Non-profit home care organisations are also increasingly training home helps to deliver personal care, i.e. de facto to combine the roles of home help and health care assistant.

Older person's entitlements and expectations have changed significantly over the last 10 years. The Medical Card was granted to all residents in Ireland aged 70 and over in 2001. This, together with population ageing, the strong preference among older persons for living in their own homes (Garavan, Winder and McGee, 2001) and the availability of home care packages in some areas (Timonen, 2004), has contributed to increased demand for home care services. Yet, considerable confusion prevails over the extent of entitlement to social care services. Lack of clear guidelines in charges for nursing home care was the subject of a major legal case in 2004-05 (see for instance O'Dell, 2006). Similar debates are yet to take place openly over the financing of care in the community, but they promise to be no less acrimonious.

Focus of this Book

Clearly, addressing all the deficits in our knowledge of community-dwelling older persons and in the provision of care to them in Ireland is not possible within the scope of one book. As it is not possible to carry out a comprehensive study on the care needs of the community-dwelling older population in the absence of a national, representative survey of older people, it was decided to focus on care *provision*. The aim of this study was to acquire an understanding of the current state of formal *in-home* care services (i.e. domiciliary care services) for older people in the Dublin area (excluding Wicklow and Kildare). The strong presence of public, non-profit and private care organisations in Dublin makes it the ideal microcosm for analysing the roles and inter-linkages between these three sectors. This study does *not* comprise community care services that are delivered outside older persons' homes or in home-like settings such as day-care centres and sheltered housing.

There are three categories of formal home care workers who deliver care and support services in the homes of older persons: home helps, health care assistants and private agency care workers. Representatives from each category and their managers were used as informants in order to draw some comparisons between the work profile, organisation and terms and conditions of employment in the public, private and non-profit sectors:

- **Public**: State sector care workers delivering home care services financed by the state through tax revenues; these are employees of the Health Services Executive (HSE) (or a subsidiary) and provide personal care exclusively.

- **Non-profit**: Care workers hired by non-profit home help organisations and paid indirectly by the State via monies that the state channels to the non-profit organisations.[3]

- **Private**: While the care services provided by private companies are in most cases privately financed, an increasing number of home care packages being made available to older persons with care needs

---

[3] Outside Dublin, home helps are in most cases directly employed by the HSE and as such tend to enjoy better terms and conditions than their counterparts in the capital.

means that the State is involved in financing these services provided by private agencies.

Figure 1.4: The Three Sectors, Primary Focus and Care Worker Titles

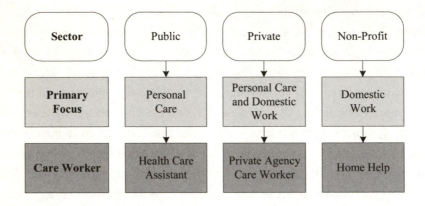

The **key research questions** addressed in this book are:

• What are the key characteristics (e.g. size, operating principles) of the three sectors (public, non-profit and private) involved in the provision of domiciliary care for older persons?

• What is the division of labour between these three sectors? Do they specialise in certain tasks and client groups?

• How are individuals working in the three sectors equipped to carry out their work?

• What are the central issues of concern firstly, for home helps, health care assistants and private agency care workers, and secondly, for private and public home care directors and key HSE employees involved in the management of home care services?

• What are the interconnections between the three sectors, both at the level of financing and strategic planning, and at the individual level?

• What kind of impact do social policies have on the structures of care provision, the quality of care, the availability of care and the experience of transitions between care delivered by different providers?

Conclusion

As was argued above, "care" is an area of gerontological research where much work remains to be done in Ireland, and internationally.[4] It is also an area where change is very rapid. While many economic aspects of ageing (pensions, labour market participation etc.) have been the long-standing subject of extensive research, the policy issues surrounding the care of older people from both a provider and user perspective have not been adequately researched to date.

This research has not been commissioned by an external body but arises from the observation (based on both current policy debates and other projects completed to date) that formal domiciliary care services are a crucial, yet under-researched, part of the Irish care regime. It is anticipated that the information and analysis contained in this book will be of relevance, interest and use to academics, students and policy analysts, but also to domiciliary care organisations in the public, non-profit and private sectors involved in the provision and financing of home care in planning their future work in this area.

---

[4] While several high-quality theoretical and empirical works have been published in the area of (community-based) long-term care services for older people, the area of care services for older people still remains under-researched. A noteworthy recent research project on care work with older people in Sweden, Spain and England was carried out within an EU Framework 5 project under the title of *Care Work in Europe: Current Understandings and Future Directions.*

Chapter 2

RESEARCH METHODS

Virpi Timonen and David Prendergast

The main aim of this research was to provide an insightful overview of the rapidly changing, under-researched and highly policy-relevant area of domiciliary care services to older people. Due to the lack of primary datasets or recent interview records, the research team had to generate virtually all of the data, primarily through semi-structured interviews with a total of 125 informants working in the area of formal domiciliary care for older people.

The study took a three-pronged approach, examining the domiciliary care of older people in Dublin from the perspective of key administrative and managerial stakeholders and the point of view of home care workers themselves, across the public, private and non-profit sectors. While there are other types of care workers delivering services to older people in the community, most notably Public Health Nurses (PHNs) and Registered General Nurses (RGNs), these categories of care workers were mainly excluded as the aim was to interview people delivering formal non-medical domiciliary care. Community-based nurses receive relatively cursory treatment in this study because they typically deliver medical care, tend to interact with older persons for short periods of time often on an irregular basis, and are professionally qualified nurses. In contrast, home care workers typically perform non-medical care tasks, have a range of different (non-medical) qualifications and generally are in more frequent direct contact with the older person.

Interviews took place across the three "pillars" of public, non-profit and private sectors, and along the three "layers" of planning/strategic/ financial management, middle (operational) management and "direct" care work (see Table 2.1 below).

Table 2.1: Home Care Services Matrix — Interviewees

	Public	**Non-Profit**	**Private**
Planning/ Strategic/Financing	Local Health Office (LHO) Manager of Services for Older Persons, LHO Director of Public Health Nursing, General Manager of LHO	N/A – though some boards were active in long term strategising, the LHO usually plays an important role here.	N/A – though some directors directly negotiated financing and planning strategies
Operational Management	Manager of Services for Older Persons, Homecare Package Coordinator, District Care Unit manager, PHNs, Directors of Public Health Nursing[1]	Home Help Organisers[2]	Private Agency/Company Directors
Care Workers	Health Care Assistants (HCA)	Home Help Workers (HH)	Private Care Workers (PCW)

Primary Sources

Statistics and Administrative Sources

Prior to the collection of interview data, statistical databases, administrative records and reports were reviewed in order to gather background information on care in the community in Ireland. The aim at this stage of

---

[1] Note that, in the public sector, there is considerable overlap in interviewees in layers 1 and 2.

[2] This is currently the most common title; however, many organisers interviewed for this study stated their dissatisfaction with the title which does not reflect their considerable management responsibilities. Consequently, many of them wish to adopt and some have adopted the title "home care manager" (see also Chapter 5).

the project was to set the scene and to establish the state of knowledge in the area. A trawl through the *Golden Pages* and world wide web was necessary to uncover information on the private sector. On the basis of the available data,[3] estimations were made of the number of domiciliary care hours provided through the non-profit sector, public expenditure on domiciliary care, and the number of private and non-profit home care organisations (see Table 2.2 below.) It must be stressed that there is very little readily-available, systematic administrative data on home care services, and that most of this has to be painstakingly excavated. While we are very grateful to all those who helped us to unearth this data, the difficulties encountered and the time spent on extracting this data are completely out of proportion, and a few simple databases, set up centrally by the HSE, should spare any future researchers (and indeed administrators, managers, politicians and others interested in the data) the trouble of hunting for this information.

Table 2.2: Summary of Relevant Figures for Dublin

• Dublin's total over-65 population at the outset of the research was 113,972 (10.15 per cent of the population of the Greater Dublin area)
• There are eight HSE LHOs in the Dublin area (excluding Wicklow and Kildare).
• 28 non-profit home care organisations[4] operated within these eight LHO areas (six additional organisations operate in Kildare and Wicklow)

---

[3] Data on home helps and health care assistants was obtained from the Department of Health and Children and from the HSE. Data/information on private sector home care agencies and non-profit home help organisations was obtained directly from some of these agencies and organisations.

[4] These organisations are sometimes referred to as "voluntary home help organisations" or as "home help organisations". Here, for reasons of clarity, we have adopted the term "non-profit home care organisation" as we believe that this term best illustrates their key characteristics, namely that they are not-for-profit and are engaged in delivering a range of home care services. As many of these organisations now employ carers performing both personal care and domestic work tasks, it is increasingly the case that the term "home help organisation" is slightly misleading. Also, the term "voluntary" is frequently misinterpreted as meaning that the home helps and personal care attendants working for these organisations are not paid: in fact, they do receive a wage and in theory, although in most cases not in practice, are covered by pension and other benefits.

- 15,150 older persons received care from the non-profit home care organisations (this is an approximate figure that refers to the greater Dublin area, i.e. it includes Wicklow and Kildare).

- Estimates based on three clients per home help equates to 5,050 home helps working for the non-profit home care organisations in Dublin.

- We estimate that 15 private home care companies operate in the geographical area that covers LHO 1–8. With a couple of exceptions, many of these at present have smaller client bases than the non-profit home care organisations, but are growing rapidly.

Interviews

Focus groups and in-depth semi-structured interviews were the primary research methods chosen for this study. The possibility of participant observation was considered, but rejected due to the considerable practical difficulties, the time investment and the ethical dilemmas involved. Meetings took place within a variety of locations ranging from focus groups held at Trinity College to interviews with small groups and individuals in health centres, private agency premises, meeting rooms in hotels, and very occasionally the homes of carers. Signed consent was gained from all participants and confidentiality procedures were carefully explained both orally and in writing prior to the start of the interview.

Sample Selection

Anecdotal evidence and preliminary interviews conducted by the authors suggested that large variations exist within Dublin in relation to the operation, scale and availability of the different types of domiciliary care services. To uncover these variations the research focused on the delivery of domiciliary services within each of the eight Dublin LHOs. Whilst significant differences in the formal domiciliary care sector exist within Ireland, Dublin is arguably the most suitable location for analysis of the characteristics of the public, private and non-profit sectors in this field, as significant levels of activity are in evidence across all three sectors in the capital.

A small number (N=5) of preparatory, intelligence-gathering interviews were conducted in the summer-autumn of 2005 with national and regional level officials from the HSE, and the relevant trade unions (SIPTU and Impact). A couple of these interviewees read and contributed to the improvement of the research proposal for this project.

At the planning/strategic/financing level, the intention was to capture all possible respondents, i.e. all managers of services for older persons and the director of public health nursing (or their assistant director) from each LHO. This aim was reached with interviews taking place in the central community care offices of each of the eight LHOs. The LHO general manager in each area was also invited to participate if they believed they had contributions to make on the subject of home care. In one of the LHO areas interviews were arranged with the home care package coordinator as well as the local district care unit team leader with the view to gaining a deeper insight into the operation of the home care packages.

At the intermediate operational management level the intention was to capture all private agency directors in Dublin. The majority of directors agreed to be interviewed for the research. Many of the private company directors were keen for their agencies to be represented in the study — indeed a couple actively contacted us in order to ensure that their views would be taken into consideration. In the case of the (much larger number of) non-profit sector home help organisers/managers, the intention was to achieve the widest possible spread of organisations across the LHO areas: in total 17 of the 28 organisations participated in the study.

Securing a representative sample at the care worker level was somewhat more complex. The size of the workforce in each of the three sectors varies considerably, and in order to explore the diversity of workers in the three sectors equally, it was decided to interview an equal number of care workers from each sector. In a study based primarily on semi-structured qualitative interviews it is clearly not possible to achieve a sample size that would be sufficient for generalising the findings across the workforce as whole. However, we estimated that conducting a minimum of 20 interviews with each category of care worker (yielding a total of 60 interviews with care workers) would ensure that the saturation point in terms of unearthing novel information and patterns would be reached. As the discussion in Chapters 4, 5 and 6 will show, it is indeed likely that such a saturation point was reached in the case of the public sector health care assistants and in the case of non-profit sector home helps. However, this was arguably not the case for private agency care workers, who were found to work in a rapidly developing industry with a distinct lack of standardisation regarding working and employment conditions.

We will now proceed to give some additional detail on the interviewees from the three layers of planning/strategic/financing informants, operational management and care workers.

Layer 1: Planning/Strategic/Financing

Table 2.3: Interviewees with Planning, Strategic and Financing Responsibilities in the Area of Home Care for Older People

Categories Interviewed	Number of People Interviewed
Manager of Services for Older People	8
Director or Assistant Director of Public Health Nursing	9
General Manager of LHO	2
National or Regional Level HSE official	2
Trade Union Representative	3
Dublin City Council official	4
Total	*28*

The primary purpose of these interviews was to gain an understanding of the home care services that are provided directly by the HSE/LHOs (i.e. the public sector), and of the links that HSE employees have with the non-profit and private home care providers in their area.

Interviews were conducted with key representatives from each of the LHO areas, yielding a total of eight research events at this level. The numbers of interviewees in each meeting ranged from two to four and were usually composed of the LHO manager of services for older people, the director of public health nursing or their relevant assistant director. In two of the cases, the LHO general manager chose to contribute, and in one meeting an additional assistant director of public health nursing attended upon her own request.

During or following the interview a number of key points of hard data were gathered, including:

- Population statistics in the LHO, including numbers of people over 65.

- Services available in the area, including numbers of health centres, home help hours, community nursing staff, health care assistants, home care packages, meals-on-wheels organisations, home care providers, supportive accommodation developments and day care facilities.

The collection of statistics was then used to facilitate a more general and wide-ranging discussion of the following dominant themes:

- Changing budgetary provision for the maintenance of older persons in their homes.

- The introduction and expansion of home care packages in the area, and the possible future impact upon the generic home help budget.

- The relationship between the HSE and the non-profit home care organisations.

- The emergence and development of the private care industry in the LHO.

- The role of the health care assistant, including issues surrounding training, Garda clearance, work tasks, and conditions of employment.

- Views on policy and recommendations for improvement.

Layer 2: Operational Management

Table 2.4: Interviewees Involved in the Operational Management of Home Care Services

Categories Interviewed	Number of People Interviewed
Non-Profit Home Help Organisers	18
Non-Profit Home Help Assistant Managers	3
Private Care Agency/Company Directors	10
Private Care Agency/Company Assistant Managers	1
Manager of a District Care Unit (DCU)	1
Coordinator of Home Care Packages	1
Total	*34*

The aim of these consultations was to provide an overview of the administrative and policy framework within which the managers and directors of home care workers operate.

Non-profit Home Care Organisations

Invitations to a series of afternoon focus group held at Trinity College were sent to 28 Home Help Organisers. The maximum number of participants in these meetings was five and the longest meeting took just under three hours. In addition to general discussions that explored recent changes in home care provision and their relationship with both the HSE and their carers, each participant was asked to give a short history of their organisation and to provide information on the numbers of home helps employed and their various operating procedures.

The following table lists the total number of non-profit home care organisations in each of the LHO areas and the number of organisers we interviewed.

Table 2.5: Interview Breakdown for Non-profit Home Care Organisations per LHO Area

LHO Area	Total Number of Home Care Organisations	Number of Home Care Organisations Interviewed
1	2	2
2	5	3
3	2*	2
4	2	0
5	3	3
6	2	1
7	7	5
8	5	2
Total	*28*	*18*

* Three of the organisations funded by area 2 also operate in the boundaries of area 3.

Focus groups were set up to bring together as many organisations as possible from within a single LHO area, however we occasionally combined the areas where this was not possible due to small numbers. This provided some interesting comparative data. Three of the organisers were interviewed individually at their premises to solve the practical difficulties of taking time off work, travelling into Trinity College or to discuss some potentially sensitive issues.

Private Agency Directors

A postal survey of private home care agencies was conducted in summer/autumn 2005. The results of this survey and the interviews are discussed in Chapter 6.

A total of ten interviews with private care agency directors were subsequently conducted. This represents a very large percentage of the private care companies operating in Dublin, and indeed in the whole country as most agencies are located in the capital. The companies we interviewed tended to primarily provide home care, though some also had links into the nursing home sector. Eight of the ten were indigenous Irish companies; two were US-based franchises that had recently opened in Dublin.

The private agency directors had to be interviewed individually for two main reasons: time constraints and fears over confidential information and loss of competitive advantage. One-on-one interviews were particularly useful in this latter regard as many directors felt they could speak more freely under agreed conditions of anonymity. Many of the questions asked of the private companies mirrored those raised with the non-profit organisations. Additional themes explored included insurance, experiences with private clients, the new home care packages, tax issues and carers as employees versus self employed workers.

Layer 3: Care Workers

Table 2.6: Interviewees Involved in Direct Provision of Care

Categories Interviewed	Number of People Interviewed
Health Care Assistants	20
Non-Profit Home Care Workers (home helps)	20
Private Agency Care Workers	23
Total	*63*

Although random cluster sampling was initially considered for the care workers interviews, it had to be abandoned due to the absence of sampling frames and the considerable difficulty involved in securing the co-operation of some employers/managers and the care workers themselves.

Of the three categories of workers, the easiest to recruit were workers from the non-profit organisations. This was due to both the sizable population of potential interviewees available and the number of organisations across Dublin. Home help organisers were asked during their own interviews if they could advertise our upcoming focus groups amongst their workforces. Three focus group afternoons were held at Trinity College during which a total of 19 workers from the three old health board areas were interviewed. The new system of LHOs was only introduced in January 2005. Prior to this, Dublin was divided up amongst health boards. LHO areas 1 and 2 were part of the old East Coast Health Board; areas 3, 4 and 5 of the South Western Health Board; and areas 6, 7 and 8 of the Northern Health Board. Interviews with both HSE personnel and home help organisers reinforced the impression that the ties between the LHO areas in these three groupings remain strong and so it was clear that this, combined with the likelihood of a wide geographical distribution, would provide a reasonable basis on which to divide up the LHOs for our three afternoons of meetings. Turnout from non-profit home care workers was generally excellent with nine participants from each grouping; with the exception of the organisations from areas 3, 4 and 5. Only two workers from this category turned up. During these afternoons, all three researchers were present allowing for several small group interviews to be held simultaneously. One worker who was unable to attend the afternoon was interviewed at her request in a one-on-one interview several days later.

Table 2.7: Interview Breakdown for Non-Profit Sector Home Care Workers per LHO Area

LHO Area	Total Number of Non Profit Home Care Workers Interviewed
1	3
2	6
3	0
4	0
5	2
6	0
7	8
8	1
Total	*20*

HSE health care assistants form a much smaller total population of workers but were generally keen to be interviewed. We were fortunate in receiving enough support and advertising from all the directors of public health nursing that we were able to recruit health care assistants from each of the eight LHOs. Interview afternoons were held at Trinity College for those health care assistants relatively close to the College or with the time to attend. Eleven workers attended our first event. We heard reports from some directors of public health nursing that their health care assistants had expressed interest in the study but that the time and distance involved had been off-putting. Consequently, efforts were made by the research team to conduct interviews with health care assistants in the health centres of the three unrepresented LHOs. The following table shows the breakdown of health care assistants interviewed.

Table 2.8: Interview Breakdown for Health Care Assistants per LHO Area

LHO Area	Total Number of HCAs Interviewed
1	2
2	2
3	3
4	2
5	1
6	3
7	2
8	5
Total	*20*

Access to private agency workers was on the whole substantially more difficult to secure. Whilst some directors of private sector agencies/ companies went to great lengths to advertise our study and request interviews amongst their workers, several preferred not to participate in this aspect of the study. Three companies attempted to advertise and actively recruit workers on our behalf, but reported back that their workers were not interested in participating. Many workers felt that their work or childcare schedules prohibited participation; others cited the distances involved, the relative lack of payment, or simply expressed disinterest in an academic study. As with the health care assistants, therefore, the interviews with private care workers were conducted in a variety of settings and times to secure access.

***Table 2.9: One-on-One and Group Interviews with Private Care
Workers: Frequency and Size of Groups***

Number of Private Care Workers in Interview Group	Frequency
1	5
2	2
3	0
4	1
5	2
Total	*10 research meetings* *23 PCWs interviewed*

A total of 23 care workers from six private companies were interviewed.
Most of the larger private organisations were represented. A particularly
ambitious event held by one company in the closing stages of fieldwork
ensured that we gained an additional three care workers on top of our
target sample of 20. As the above table demonstrates a substantial number of the workers from the private sector were interviewed alone or in
very small groups. This mixed approach of combining the focus group
method with in-depth one to one interviews was particularly advantageous in light of the large number of issues raised in the interviews relating to this emerging industry.

The following information was obtained through all the care worker
and health care assistant interviews:

- Gender, nationality of care worker

- Job title/description

- Relevant training and qualifications, monitoring/supervision

- Recruitment pathway and reasons for entering line of work

- Duration of care work (to date and projected)

- Typical working time and care tasks performed

- Level of and factors contributing to/undermining job satisfaction

- Terms and conditions: employment status, salary, social rights, holiday entitlements, in-kind benefits

- Union membership

- Relationship with care recipients

- Relationship with other care workers

- Perceived challenges and problems, policy suggestions.

These questions are relevant for gaining an understanding of the profile of care workers, factors that attract people to this type of work, influence worker retention rates, and also the insights that care workers have gained into the impact of different policies and practices on the well-being of their clients.

Interview Totals

As can be seen from Table 2.10, a total of 125 informants were consulted in the course of a total of 55 research events.

Table 2.10: Total Number of Interviewees and Research Events

Level	Number of Participants	Number of Research Meetings
Planning and Financing	28	13
Operational Management	34	21
Care Workers	63	21
Total	*125*	*55*

Data

The interview material was written up and coded into dominant themes for each category of workers. Data analysis was done both manually and with the aid of the QSR N6 Qualitative Data Analysis software programme. This yielded information and analysis on a number of key areas, including:

- Overall organisation of home care services in the Dublin area

- Key similarities and differences between the three sectors

- Tasks expected from and performed by the different categories of care workers and their organisers/managers, their working patterns, recruitment pathways, remuneration and benefits, relationship with clients

- The influence of the policy and organisational environment on the different types of care worker and their managers

- The inter-relationships between the three different areas/sectors (public, private and non-profit) of home care provision

- The aspects of care policy that are perceived to be positive/negative.

Chapter Structure

For the purposes of analysis and presentation, the interview data is divided into three sections, namely State, non-profit and private, and Chapters 4, 5 and 6 address these respectively. Prior to these chapters, Chapter 3 sets out a brief history of home care provision in Ireland, and also discusses the key principles underpinning the Irish care service regime. Chapter 7 compares the three sectors, and Chapter 8 sketches out the policy challenges that remain to be addressed. Chapter 9 concludes.

Chapter 3

THE HISTORICAL AND SYSTEMIC CONTEXT

Virpi Timonen and Martha Doyle

Care of older persons in their own homes has in recent years received much attention in Ireland. The reasons for this are many, and the proponents of domiciliary care are able to draw on both "hard" (economic) and "soft" (quality of life) arguments. However, little detailed analysis of the historical background and the changing meaning of key concepts in the area of formal home care has been presented to date. This chapter seeks to fill this gap by addressing the historical evolution of the emphasis on community care and the changing meaning of key organising principles such as subsidiarity.

It is frequently asserted that domiciliary care, as opposed to institutional care, is the preferred choice of most older people in Ireland, and there is evidence that this is indeed the case (Garavan, Winder and McGee, 2001; O'Hanlon et al., 2005; McGee et al., 2005). Furthermore, it appears, in the light of data from HeSSOP, that roughly equal proportions of older persons find informal (family) and formal care (provided by the state, the non-profit sector and the private sector) acceptable. This contradicts the cherished myth that all older persons only want their own relatives to care for them. However, it is important to acknowledge at the outset that both historically and at present, the care of older persons in their own homes is in most cases provided by relatives and friends. The importance of enabling older persons with care needs to remain living in their own homes (even in the absence of a supportive informal carer network), has come to be strongly emphasised in Irish social policy. The *Care of the Aged Report* of 1968 (produced by the Inter-Departmental Committee on the Care of the Aged) stressed the desirability of domiciliary or "community" care, both from the point of view of the older person's well-being and from a cost perspective (i.e. the direct costs to the public purse, not necessarily the opportunity and other costs incurred by informal carers).

Despite this recent and growing emphasis on domiciliary care (especially the current attention on home care packages), it is important to recognise that this is relatively recent, and to trace the movement in policy terms away from an emphasis on institutional care. This chapter analyses the emergence of this focus on home care, the different forms that policies and practices around the homecare of older persons have taken and the most significant recent changes in the principles underlying home care policy and provision. The chapter will conclude with a discussion of the potential contribution that formal care services providers can make towards the aim of enabling the maximum number of older persons with care needs to remain living in their homes for as long as they wish.

Changes in Key Features of Home Care Provision

Three central features of Irish care policy have undergone major changes over the last 10 years:

Subsidiarity

The notion of subsidiarity is an elementary principle of the Catholic Church's social teaching. The principle of subsidiarity was developed in the encyclical *Rerum Novarum* of 1891 by Pope Leo XIII and was further developed in Pope Pius XI's encyclical *Quadragesimo Anno* of 1931. The "fundamental", "unshaken" and "unchangeable" [Catholic] principle of subsidiarity is spelled out in *Quadragesima Anno* (1931: § 79, 80) as follows:[1]

---

[1] The principle of subsidiarity is defined and spelled out in various other papal encyclicals such as the *Rerum Novarum* e.g. (§ 10): "the domestic household is antecedent, as well in idea as in fact, to the gathering of men into a community".

> [I]t is an injustice, a great evil and a disturbance of right order,
> for a large and higher association to arrogate to itself functions
> which can be performed efficiently by smaller and lower so-
> cieties. . . . The State . . . should leave to smaller groups the
> settlement of business of minor importance, which otherwise
> would greatly distract it; it will thus carry out with greater
> freedom, power and success the tasks belonging to it alone,
> because it alone can effectively accomplish these: directing,
> watching, stimulating, restraining, as circumstances suggest
> and necessity demands.

A logical application of the subsidiarity principle to the context of social
care dictates that care should be provided, whenever possible, by the social unit closest to the person in need of care. In the first instance, this
means the family and other informal carers. As Convery writes (2001, p.
83):

> Traditionally, the family has taken most responsibility for the
> care of frail older people in Ireland, and this is still the expec-
> tation. Although adults are not legally obliged to care for their
> parents or other elderly relatives, there is an implied moral ob-
> ligation placed on them to do so, whenever possible.

This tendency to rely on the family as the primary provider of care for
older people has formed, Convery (*op. cit.*) argues, the foundation of
government policy leading to "the gross underdevelopment of [formal]
community services for older people living at home". As the discussion
below will show, the principle of subsidiarity was not adhered to during
the early phase in the development of care services for older persons in
Ireland. The institutional care that was originally the only option available to older persons in need of formal care services was dominated by
the State both in the financer and provider roles (e.g. most county homes
were state-run).

As the care regime in Ireland gradually started to shift towards community-based solutions, the subsidiarity principle became more visible in
practice. However, the precise meaning of subsidiarity has changed radically over time and its practical manifestations have been anything but
unchangeable. At first, voluntary organisations provided care services

largely unaided by the government (i.e. genuinely "voluntarily"), subsequently the state started to support them financially, and more recently government regulations are turning the workers in this sector
(originally volunteers, then very badly paid workers) into something
approximating a public sector worker. For this reason, it is now more
accurate to refer to this sector as "non-profit" rather than "voluntary"
as virtually all employees/workers are paid.

Even more importantly, government financing is beginning to flow
towards private sector providers as well. The rise of the private sector
home care business over the last 10–15 years, and its recent rapid expansion, is a highly significant development that has its origins both in the
limited funding made available to the public and non-profit sectors and
in the increased emphasis on public-private partnerships where public
funds are used to purchase home care services from private companies.
While this extension of the provider role to the private sector is arguably
a logical augmentation of the subsidiarity principle, it has given rise to a
number of questions regarding the State's accountability and responsibility, and as Chapter 6 in particular shows, these are yet to be satisfactorily
addressed in the Irish context.

Universal versus Residual Entitlements

As the discussion below will highlight, the history of formal service provision was characterised by residual (means-tested) entitlements reserved
for the poorest. As a result of the extension of medical cards to all persons aged 70 and over in 2001, all residents in this cohort are in principle
entitled to publicly provided home care services (delivered by health care
assistants) for free. The scarcity of services means that they are in practice typically entitled to one to two hours per week in many areas. Furthermore, the medical card has created the impression among many older
people and families that the services delivered by non-profit organisations (home help) are also free. In practice, our research has shown that
many organisations ask for contributions that can amount to more than
50 per cent of the costs of delivering the service. As with health care assistant services, home help is typically restricted to an hour or two per
day, which is clearly not sufficient for individuals with extensive care

needs. As a result, the role of families in providing care remains prominent, and the role of privately financed services is getting stronger.

Role of Church and Religious Orders

Historically, the role of the Church in the development of care services in Ireland was clearly predominant, as the discussion below will show. Many non-profit home help organisations still have religious on their boards, but these people typically exercise less power in practice than they had done previously. Moreover, many non-profit organisations that now compete with the emerging private sector seem to be evolving into limited companies with more professional boards and management structures. This, combined with the rather static nature of the non-profit sector in comparison with the rapidly expanding private sector, means that the role of the religious orders and their representatives is shrinking and can now be characterised as rather marginal in the Irish care services regime.

The Role and Extent of Informal Care

Another area that is frequently claimed to have changed is the role and extent of informal care-giving. While we do know that the bulk of care to community-dwelling older persons is provided informally, i.e. by unpaid family members, relatives and friends, we have only very limited understanding about the extent of such informal care provision. The 2001 Census collected information on the number of informal/family carers, but these are not broken down by client group. As a result it is not possible to estimate what proportion of them care for children or adults with disabilities as opposed to older persons (although it is defensible to conjecture that at least two-thirds of the persons receiving informal care are aged 65 or over). Furthermore, there is considerable uncertainty regarding the number, needs and circumstances of the "heavy duty" informal carers, i.e. those who are providing care for more than 43 hours per week. As Table 3.1 below shows, 66.7 per cent of these carers are women, but once again we cannot be sure what proportion of them care for older adults. An educated guess is two-thirds, yielding nearly 27,000 full-time informal carers looking after older people in Ireland. We therefore currently lack the information for assessing accurately the extent and nature of informal care in the community.

Table 3.1: Carers in Ireland by Number of Hours of Unpaid Help Provided

Hours per Week	Men	Women	% Women
1-14	34,975	49,887	58.8
15-28	5,863	9,547	62.0
29-42	3,142	4,815	60.5
43+	13,501	27,025	66.7
Total carers	57,480	91,274	61.4

Source: Census 2001 (CSO).

We will now turn to a brief exposition of the history of formal service provision for older persons in Ireland, and examine the transition in this area from the overwhelming emphasis on institutional care delivered by the State and by religious and voluntary organisations, to an increasing emphasis, at least rhetorically, on domiciliary care delivered by a wider range of (predominantly non-state) providers.

Brief History of Formal Service Provision for Older Persons in Ireland: From Institutionalisation to Domiciliary Care

The earliest forms of publicly provided care for the aged were institutional, and were not specifically designed for older persons but rather the poor, the sick and various categories of people who were deemed deviant ("sturdy beggars", disorderly women and orphan children). The Act of Irish Parliment 1703 provided for the setting up of a House of Industry in Dublin. Subsequent Acts in 1735, 1752 and 1772 resulted in the construction of similar Houses of Industry in Cork, Belfast, north Dublin and Clonmel. The House of Industry in North Brunswick Street Dublin housed 888 "aged and infirm" poor persons, along with 474 "incurable lunactics" and epileptics and 303 sick persons. A similar complex was built in South Dublin (James Street) which housed 250 "aged and infirm" males and 350 "aged and infirm" females (Higginbotham, 2003). The Poor Relief Act of 1838 led to the establishment of these institutions on a larger scale. From the start, workhouses operated on a residual principle, i.e. they were reserved for the poorest and indeed were purposefully designed to be so austere as to "attract" only those who had nowhere else to go.

The Vice-Regal Commission on Poor Law Reform in 1906 recommended the establishment of County Alms Houses in order to better cater for the aged and the infirm. Their needs were poorly looked after in the workhouses as these combined a large array of individuals with very diverse needs. While the recommendations of this commission were not followed, the workhouses were in many areas gradually consolidated into a single "County Home", with the intention that these would become more focused on the aged and infirm destitute. In practice, however, poor provision for other groups in need of shelter and assistance meant that County Homes continued to cater for a very mixed population. Before the introduction, in 1909, of the non-contributory old age pension (a means-tested payment for persons aged 70 or over), destitute older persons without relatives or friends usually had no choice but to enter a workhouse or County Home. Despite attempts to improve conditions in County Homes in the post-war period, the range of inhabitants remained wide, including people with intellectual disabilities and even children, in addition to the chronically ill, most of whom were aged 65 or over (Inter-Departmental Committee on the Care of the Aged 1968, p. 32). Following the foundation of the Irish Free State and subsequent Irish Civil War many workhouses had undergone military occupation and had been damaged or burnt down. Of those that remained, 33 became County Homes offering relief to the elderly and chronic invalids, 32 became District Fever Hospitals and nine became County Hospitals (Higginbotham, 2003).

The early stages of public provision for older persons in Ireland are therefore focused on institutional care for the very poorest. In other words, historically formal care for the aged in Ireland was institutional and residual (means-tested) in character. Help and support for older persons living in their own homes developed much later. The logical explanation for this delay in the development of domiciliary care lies in the fact that all care and help in the private sphere of a home was assumed to originate in the kin and neighbourhood network. The Poor Relief Act of 1847 made provisions for "outdoor relief", but this took the form of material assistance in-kind and for this reason cannot very well be construed as an early form of community care. "Home assistance" for the aged and infirm became available at a later stage, and in addition to monetary aid consisted of extra allowances for fuel during the winter months, clothing and footwear, spectacles, artificial limbs and so on (Society of St Vincent de Paul, 1942). Home Assistance was the precursor of the modern "free schemes" (television licence, telephone rental, electricity allowance, travel passes) that are now available to older persons in Ireland on a universal basis.

Two religious orders that had played a particularly prominent role in setting up the first organised community care services in Dublin were the Litte Sisters of the Poor and the Little Sisters of the Assumption. The Congregation of the Little Sisters of the Assumption, based at the Convent of the Assumption in Camden street (established in 1891), "devoted themselves exclusively to the nursing of the Sick Poor in their homes". Similar work looking after the sick poor was carried out from another convent in York Road, Dun Laoghaire (established in 1897), extending to the areas of Glasthule, Blackrock and Monkstown (*The Irish Catholic Registry and Almanac,* 1954). The *Social Workers' Handbook,* published in Dublin in the mid-1940s by the Society of St. Vincent de Paul (1942), refers to the "nursing of the sick poor in their own homes . . . without restriction of age or sex", carried out by the Little Sisters of the Assumption from their bases in Camden Street and Dun Laoghaire. The entry in this handbook also states that "no payment is accepted" for this service. However, it specifies that "[c]hronic cases are not accepted but ordinary illness, even if long continued, is looked after". It is possible that this provison excluded many older clients (Society of St Vincent de Paul, undated publication circa 1944). Other congregations that are listed as offering home nursing include the Sisters of Bon Secours (Westland Row), Brothers of St Vincent de Paul Society, Legionaries of Mary, Members of the Solidarity of Our Lady and the Sisters of Mercy.

In 1881, the Congregation of the Little Sisters of the Poor founded a care institution for "respectable poor aged people, male and female" in Kilmainham. In the mid-1950s, there were 320 people resident in this home (*Irish Catholic Registry and Almanac,* 1954). This order also operated a "home for poor aged people, male and female", founded in 1944 and housing 150 persons in the mid-1950s. Some 130 older persons were resident at the St. Joseph's asylum for aged females in the mid-1950s, which was run by the Congregation of the Poor Servants of the Mother of God.

Home nursing seemed to have been more developed than home care. Home nursing services were set up at the beginning of the twentieth century by the Queen's Institute of District Nursing in Ireland and the Lady Dudley Nursing Scheme. As well as delivering services under the Maternity and Child Welfare and Tuberculosis Schemes, they delivered care to the "chronic sick and other sick persons" (Department of Health Files, 1937–1963). Local committees helped to inform the nurses of potential clients. The Queen's Institute of Nursing established itself by first creating small area committees who would collect sufficient funds to cover the expenses of a nurse in the community. Nurses were subsequently furnished with a house or lodgings and in some instances a car. The Superintendent of the Queen's Institute monitored their work in the various districts. The Lady Dudley service was established to service the areas which the Queen's Institute had failed to cover, namely poorer areas, including counties Cork, Kerry, Galway, Mayo, Sligo and Donegal. Once again local fund-raising committees were created to finance the placement of the nurses. Supervision of the Lady Dudley nurses was also undertaken by the Queen's Institute. In 1951 there were 161 nurses employed by the Queen's Institute and 48 employed by the Lady Dudley nursing scheme. In total, these voluntary organisations covered approximately one-third of the country (Department of Health Files, 1937-1963). Section 102 of the Health Act of 1947 empowered but did not oblige the health authorities to make arrangements for the provision of home nurses. The activities of the Queen's Institute and the Lady Dudley Scheme were phased out and gradually integrated with the services of the statutory authorities coinciding with the introduction of the new position of "public health nurse" (PHN) or formerly "district nurse" in 1958. The role of the PHN became the subject of debate, culminating in a ministerial circular in 1966 specifying the responsibilities of the PHN, which among many others included domiciliary nursing (Commission on Nursing, 1988).

Although technically the health authorities were empowered to provide home nursing, the demand for such services was not adequately catered for. The utility of a home help who would provide domestic care was also beginning to be recognised. In his annual report for the year 1960, the County Medical Officer of Health [Galway], commenting on the provision of home care services, stated that:

> Most of the nurses employed wholly or partly by the County Council are in the Connemara area. Their work of necessity must deal with sick, expectant mothers and children, and no time is available for attendance to the aged. . . . Such old people need some domestic help, and I suggest that if such was given it would reduce the demand of this age group on the hospital and County Home . . . the appointment of a district home help to give twice weekly attention to such persons, to do their washing, clean their houses, cook a meal, would go to make life tolerable for such aged group. Ten or twelve such houses could be catered for by one such home help with much less cost than would be incurred by maintenance in an institution. (Department of Health Files, 1961)

The diverse and fragmented nature of voluntary sector community care services in the post-war period is evident from the following description included in the *Care of the Aged* Report (Inter-Departmental Committee on the Care of the Aged 1968, pp. 43–44):

> In addition to providing hospitals and homes a number of voluntary organisations, including religious bodies, provide non-institutional services for the aged . . . some deal only with limited services, e.g. the supply of meals, others provide a variety of services; some operate on a national basis, others operate only in certain areas; some operate on their own, some in conjunction with other bodies. . . . It would be impossible within the limits of this report to give a full picture of the range and variety of the work of every organisation . . .

Appendix 1 of the Care of the Aged Report (1968) lists 28 voluntary organisations that were "national", i.e. providing services in different locations throughout the country. These include, *inter alia*, the Catholic Women's Federation, Irish Countrywomen's Association, Irish Sisters of Charity, Little Sisters of the Assumption, Little Sisters of the Poor, National Association of the Aged, Presentation Sisters, Sisters of Bon Secours, Sisters of Charity of St. Vincent de Paul, Sisters of the Little Company of Mary, Sisters of Mercy and Society of St Vincent de Paul.

An example of one such voluntary organisation delivering home care to older people was St. Brendan's Ladies After-Care Committee (Legion of Mary). This Committee was established in 1938. Members of the organisation were recruited from friends and contacts of the Committee. In 1960 it was reported that 90 per cent of the Committee were employed in various occupations, including offices, shops and the Civil Service. Clients referrals were supplied by the St Brendan's Hospital Medical staff who met with the Committee every Wednesday evening to discuss the particulars of prospective clients. Frequently houses had to be cleaned in advance of a person's discharge from hospital. In one such instance "a two-roomed cottage in county Dublin had to get a complete overhaul which was carried out by members of the Committee giving up two successive Saturday afternoons to work" (Department of Health Files, 1937–1963). The number of visits a client received depended on the client's living arrangements and health. Older people living alone were given most attention and when ill were visited twice daily, often for long periods. Care given included domestic cleaning, food preparation and laundry, assistance with filling out entitlement forms and relaying information on same was also regarded as being of prime importance. An annual grant of £12 rising to £18 in 1956 was paid by the Department of Health to this committee to cover out-of-pocket expenses incurred by the volunteers (Department of Health Files, 1937–1963).

Although the relationship between the hospitals and the state developed from the 1930s it was not until 1953 that other health care and social voluntary services were granted special privileges (Donoghue, 2001). Under the 1953 Health Act, Section 65, a health authority, with the approval of the Minister, was permitted to give assistance "to any body which provides a service similar or ancillary to a service which the health authority may provide". This assistance would include contributions to the expenses incurred by the organisation; the supply of fuel, light, food, water and other commodities; and permit the organisation to use premises maintained by the health authority, including the supply of furniture and subsequent maintenance. It has been argued that these Section 65 grants lacked clarity and consistency, with longer established organisations being more successful in securing them (Duffy, 2003). Donoghue (1988) notes that these grants are made on a discretionary basis by service level agreements as opposed to contractual agreements which are more formal and binding. In the absence of stable long-term funding the viability of many of these organisations becomes uncertain. According to Goodwin (1997), this relationship of uncertainty, requiring annual applications for funding places a considerable strain on the organisations and in some instances has resulted in services being closed for periods. In reaction to such cut-backs, a number of organisations increased charges to recipients.

A departure from subsidiarity *strictu sensu* had clearly taken place at the central policy-making level by the time the 1968 *Care of the Aged* report was published. This report recommended that:

> [H]ealth authorities should arrange for a home help service. Where the service is operated by voluntary bodies, health authorities should contribute towards the cost involved (Inter-Departmental Committee on the Care of the Aged, 1968, p. 15).

This sentence implies that services could in principle be directly provided by the state (health authorities). Nonetheless, the report does urge health authorities to "encourage and . . . support, financially, voluntary bodies providing services for the aged".

The passing of the 1970 Health Act was of significant importance to the future of the home care industry. Whilst it made provision of home nursing mandatory, provision of home care services was at the discretion of the health boards (which were established by this act). These new health boards were also given responsibility for the Section 65 grants. Explicit reference to the provision of home help was contained in this Act. Section 61 entitled "Home Help Service" empowered a health board to make arrangements to assist in the maintenance at home of "a sick or infirm person or dependent of such a person, . . . and a person who, but for provision of a service under this section would require to be maintained otherwise than home". The chief executive officer of the board had the power to determine whether eligibility would be granted, "without charge or at such a charge as he considers appropriate". Section 26 empowered health boards to make arrangements with bodies (including voluntary bodies) to provide services under the Health Act of 1947 and 1970 to eligible persons. Section 60 of the same act obliged the health board to offer home nursing services to eligible persons and such other categories of persons specified by the minister.

Whilst not obligatory, from the late 1970s the provision of home care funded through the health boards expanded. Between 1978 and 1993 there was an increase of 252 per cent in the number of home care recipients (Brady, 1994). Between 1980 and 1993 expenditure on home help services almost doubled, with the number of home helps increasing from 5,000 in 1978 to more than 10,500 in 1993 (Brady, 1994). The *Years Ahead* report (Working Party on Services for the Elderly, 1988) stated that half of the home helps provided care via the voluntary organisations with funding from health boards; the remaining home helps were employed directly by the health board. However, the balance of this varied across the different health boards. Total expenditure on home help services in 1987 was IR£7.65 million.

In 1980 an addendum to the 1968 *Care of the Aged* report was published (Inter-Departmental Committee on the Care of the Aged, 1980). This report recommended that monitoring of home help services should be practiced when health payments are given. The preferable method of payment for home help services was also considered. In essence the 1980 Research Committee advocated the payment of cash benefits, whereby the older person "should himself be put in possession of funds to use as he choose, so that he could himself pay the home help organised by the Board or make other private arrangements" (p. 15). The Committee also advocated the introduction of a supplementary payment in the upper limit of £50 a week. It was argued that such courageous action would "tilt the balance of need away from institutional service toward community service" (Inter-Departmental Committee on the Care of the Aged, 1980, p. 15).

The Years Ahead report (Working Party on Services for the Elderly, 1988) contained a recommendation that the health boards should be obliged to provide or make arrangements to maintain persons at home, and that expansion of the home help service to include evening and weekend work was required. In addition, it recommended that neighbours providing care should be entitled to payment by the health boards. A review of the implementations of the recommendations of the *Years Ahead* report was made in 1997. Nine years later it seemed that there was "considerable uncertainty over the future course of the home nursing and home help services" (Ruddle, Donoghue and Mulvihill, 1997, reference no. 60). The view was that the "role of the Public Health Nurses and Home Helps may also change significantly in the future following reviews presently being carried out by the Department of Health" (Ruddle, Donoghue and Mulvihill, 1997, reference no. 60). The National Council on Ageing and Older People, eager to safe guard the future of the home help service, recommended that the legislative basis for the service be amended to make it the mandatory responsibility of the health board to provide or have this service provided to designated categories of old people. The Council stressed that the home help service should be available to older people whether an informal carer was available or not. The function of the health care assistants was specified as providing intensive care at home following discharge from hospital, but the home help service should be able to provide routine personal care over longer periods.

The fragmented structure of home help provision across the country (which persists to the present) was raised at a National Council for the Elderly conference on home help in 1994 (Lundstrom and McKeown, 1994). According to this conference report, there were six delivery models of the home help services, the most common model being the employment of a home help organiser by the health board, who subsequently recruits and places home helpers with clients. Sixty-five per cent of home care recipients were reported as receiving their home help services directly from the health board. Voluntary organisations predominated in the Eastern Health Board, North Western Health Board and Mid-Western Health Board. Delivery of services also varied depending on location, with home helps in four of the health boards performing substantial amounts of personal care, something not practiced in the other six health boards. Eligibility for home help was also found to vary depending on location. In some areas the medical card determined eligibility, in others it was determined by the medical card plus a means test, while in others areas the community welfare officer determined eligibility with the completion of an overall means test. The practice of charging clients also varied. In some health boards clients were encouraged to make a contribution. In others it was mandatory with the payment either given to the home helper directly or collected by the home helper on behalf of the health board. In two health boards, contributions by clients served to reduce funding by the health board.

Establishment of the care assistant role in the early-mid 1990s was of great significance since it was the first time that publicly financed *and* publicly provided (non-medical) home care services were introduced in Ireland. The most recent development, to which this book devotes considerable attention, is the private sector agencies and the delivery of their services financed by the State. The so-called cash-for-care model where the State continues to adopt an arm's length approach persists, except now funding streams to private sector companies have also been opened.

Conclusion: Role of Formal Services in Meeting Future Care Needs

It is clear that, despite their secondary position (after informal care), formal home care services constitute an increasingly important part of any strategy to enable continued residence at home when care needs emerge. While the (rhetorical) emphasis on formal care in the community has existed for several decades (e.g. the 1968 *Care of the Aged* report argues repeatedly that "it is better, and probably much cheaper, to help the aged live in the community than to provide for them in hospitals or other institutions" (Inter-Departmental Committee on the Care of the Aged, 1968, p. 10)), it has become particularly strong in the last couple of years. This heightened attention to home care (which undoubtedly arose first and foremost because of concerns about the escalating costs of hospital and other institutional care) is naturally welcome, as long as formal community care is of high quality and the option of residential care remains open, where deemed more appropriate by the care recipients themselves. As this chapter has discussed, the earliest forms of formal care for older persons in Ireland were institutional, and did not adhere to the subsidiarity principle as they were mostly financed and delivered by the State. Somewhat paradoxically, it appears that as Ireland becomes less characterised by the Catholic Church and faith, the principle of subsidiarity comes to the fore more clearly. The current trend towards cash-for-care (home care packages) is a prime example of the arm's length attitude that the subsidiarity principle recommends the State take. However, one important component of the subsidiarity principle, i.e. the duty of the State to monitor the quality of care, is yet to be realised in Ireland.

Home care is not static in either theory or practice, and can take many different forms. What are the characteristics of the private, public and non-profit sector involvement in the care of older persons in their own homes? What is the potential of the formal home care services sector in Ireland to meet the increased demand for formal in-home care services? What kind of legislation, quality standards and employment protections for the care workers are needed? These are some of the questions that the following chapters will strive to answer.

Chapter 4

THE STATE: ROLE IN THE FINANCING AND PROVISION OF HOME CARE

David Prendergast

This chapter reviews the ongoing development of the home care system from the perspective of the planners, managers and health care assistants in the HSE local health offices throughout the Dublin city area. It explores current financing of services by the public sector and the extent of its collaboration with non-profit and private home care organisations in terms of provision. The primary focus is on three key aspects: the role of the community nursing services and the health care assistant in the direct provision of home care services, the funding of the generic home help budget and the introduction of the home care package system.

Prior to the restructuring of the health boards and the formation of the HSE in January 2005, the city of Dublin was primarily served by three health board areas: East Coast, South Western and Northern[1]. These were further subdivided into community care areas and were renamed Local Health Office (LHO) areas[2] with the creation of the HSE. Demographic information relating to the eight Dublin LHOs is outlined in Table 4.1 below.

---

[1] These three boards were themselves integrated under the Eastern Regional Health Authority (ERHA).

[2] Hereafter called LHOs.

Table 4.1: Population size of LHOs in Dublin (2002)

Pre-2005 Health Board	East Coast		South Western			Northern			Totals
LHO area	1	2	3	4	5	6	7	8	
Total Population	128,814	105,068	130,494	145,765	125,747	165,710	126,207	247,000	1,174,805
Population over 65	17,184	12,730	12,949	13,660	9054	14,828	16,160	17,815	114,380
Percentage of pop. over 65	13.3%	12.1%	9.9%	9.4%	7.2%	9.0%	12.8%	7.2%	9.7%

The data for this table was provided by the managers of services for older people in each of the LHOs and is drawn from the 2002 census.[3]

The information in Table 4.1 visibly demonstrates the differences in demographics between the eight areas. Dublin in general has considerably fewer people over the age of 65 than the 11.2 per cent average for Ireland. However, LHO areas 1, 2 and 7 stand out as having relatively high numbers of older persons as a proportion of their total population. In terms of the distribution of wealth across Dublin, the use of small area population statistics to assess relative affluence and deprivation by Haase and Pratschke (2005) would suggest that areas 1 and 2, which include the environs of Sandyford, Blackrock, Killiney, Foxrock and Dun Laoghaire, score very highly on the affluent scale whilst an area such as LHO 7 has a far more mixed assortment of scores.

As noted, there are several LHOs that are substantially below the national older population average of 11.2 per cent. Indeed, only 7.2 per cent of the population of areas 5 and 8 are over the age of 65. Discrepancies like this are created, among other developments, by the rapid growth of towns such as Lucan in area 5 which house many families of working age. Area 8 is by far the largest LHO in Dublin both in terms of population and geography and stretches from Raheny and Coolock to Balbriggan and Naul on the northern borders of County Dublin. Consequently it has the largest proportion of (semi-)rural inhabitants of all the LHO areas involved in this study.

As noted in Chapter Two, this project chose to focus on the eight Dublin LHO areas. In each of these administrative districts, interviews were held with the manager of services for older people, the director of public health nursing and/or one of their assistant directors. The statistical data provided in this chapter was collected individually from managers in each of the areas. The home help data was calculated from the quarterly returns sent to the LHOs by the local non-profit home help organisations. No centralised public data service that collects and collates

---

[3] At the time of the interviews and writing, the 2002 Census was the most up-to-date source of population data available to the managers. We therefore had to rely on these 2002 figures about the numbers of people in each LHO area during comparisons with more recent data about numbers of nurses, health care assistants, home help hours etc from 2005/6.

these figures is yet in place. Initiatives to create a minimum data set that would include information about home help hours and the number of persons in receipt of home care packages, day-care, and nursing home subventions are outlined in the 2006 *HSE Service Plan*.

Community Nursing Services

At each LHO level interview, a public health nursing representative was asked for a breakdown of their numbers of health centres (see Figure 4.1), community-based nurses[4] and health care assistants. Follow-up contact was made in March 2006 to establish the exact number of Whole Time Equivalents (WTEs) actively working at that point in time (see Table 4.2). This was considered the most balanced way of assessing staff levels as the basic count of nurses is misleading due to the varied numbers of hours worked. We asked for numbers of active WTEs because this is the count of staff on the ground. Several LHOs had positions within their quotas of nurses which they had been unable to fill or were in the process of filling following resignations, retirements, career breaks, maternity or parental leave, etc. One example of this is in area 5 which at the time of research had only 31.5 Whole Time Equivalents of its complement of 43 WTE Public Health Nurses (PHNs) filled.

The current system of nursing has existed since the introduction of the District Care Unit (DCU) at the start of the 1990s as a means of integrating services and providing intensive short-term (6 to 12 weeks) rehabilitative care to (older) people discharged from hospital. Community-based RGNs and the health care assistant role were both introduced around this time, though it should be noted that the health care assistant

---

[4] One PHN director explained the distinction between the PHN and RGN as follows: the PHN has triple qualifications to cover the strata of age groups which they will be in contact with, which includes qualifications as RGN, as registered midwife and Diploma in Public Health Nursing. Their job role also includes health promotion and involves schools visits and screening programs. The Community RGN on the other hand has general nurse qualifications and works in collaboration with the PHN — their job usually consists of the delivery of clinical nursing duties, e.g. insertion of catheters, wound dressing etc. One director suggested that many of the PHNs in her area are now dealing almost exclusively with children and acting mainly in a supervisory capacity with respect to older people. The RGNs in the LHO on the other hand work largely with older people.

role has in many cases moved away from the DCU as the positions became attached to specific health centres.

Figure 4.1: Number of Health Centres by LHO in Dublin, 2006

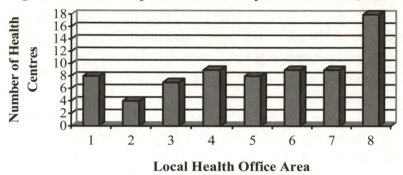

Local Health Office Area

Table 4.2: Distribution of Community Nursing (PHN and RGN) Staff (WTE) in Dublin, 2006

LHO Area	1	2	3	4	5	6	7	8	Totals
PHN	36	28	36.5	34	31.5	46.17	37.12	44	293.29
RGN	16.5	12	18.5	11.5	9.5	30.47	13.7	33.3	145.47

Directors of public health nursing usually found it difficult to accurately assess what proportion of a PHN's time would be spent working with older persons. Two directors estimated that 50 per cent of their PHNs' time was spent with older people and that work with mothers and young children increasingly requires substantial amounts of work-time. Others noted that increases in longevity as well as the numbers of older people continuing to reside in the community into late old age is leading to a corresponding rise in clinical care loads. It was also asserted that hospital discharge times have quickened, further contributing to rising demand for their services.

Beyond actual clinical care, much of the work of the PHN involves assessment or re-assessment of clients for the purposes of obtaining home care services. Occasionally clients are referred from the community but the majority arise from needs assessments made following a

hospital discharge. Complaints were made that though in theory community nurses are also supposed to provide a preventative surveillance system, this was not practically possible at the moment, considering the increasing demand for their services and the continuing restrictions placed
on the recruitment of additional health service staff. It is worth noting
here that this point, made in interviews held towards the end of 2005,
echoes the failed recommendations made 17 years prior in the *Years
Ahead* report (Working Party on Services for the Elderly, 1988), when it
was suggested that ideally PHNs would provide an anticipatory care service. The 1997 review of the implementation of this report by Ruddle,
Donoghue and Mulvihill (1997) recognised that this was not practical
under the contemporaneous resource structures, because of time constraints, poor screening schemes and the slow development of appropriate enabling technologies, but once again advocated regular screening as
a worthwhile ambition of the health services.

The employment embargo, referred to above, means that no new positions can be established in the public sector. Unless someone retires,
leaves or takes a leave of absence they have to work within the complement of current staff. As a consequence, in many areas, the provision of
a "twilight service" where evening care is provided by community nurses
or health care assistants has been phased out or not developed. As one
director of public health nursing put it:

> We ran a twilight service for years but because we did not have
> enough staff, the nurses were exhausted so the scheme was
> phased out. Subsequently the decision was made that unless the
> person is terminally ill such a service would not be offered. For
> such a scheme to be viable you need a dedicated team.

The restrictions and limited capacity created by nursing staff shortages
were discussed by most of the directors interviewed. Additional impedi-
ments cited included the introduction of the four-year degree in nursing,
which reduced the number of student nurses available to work in the
hospitals and put pressure on the community nursing service, and an increase in specialisations within the nursing field resulting in fewer people entering or remaining in·the public health nursing area. An interviewee explained that:

In the past there were very few pathways, you could either go
into management, or stay as you were, whereas now there are
loads of different specialities. This is very good but it does
leave gaps in the general workforce. It impacts on the community in a huge way . . . also you can't come into the community
off a college course; you need experience as you'll be working
alone a great deal.

One director suggested that the field of public health nursing was considerably more attractive in the 1980s than now and this is leading to an imbalance in the numbers of older PHNs, with many approaching retirement.
Expensive house prices and the cost of living in Dublin were also presented as reasons for many nurses not wishing to work in the capital. The
reorganisation of the HSE as a national body has enabled a system of easy
transfer for some nurses, which one director claimed was worrying considering the time invested in the training of new PHNs on the ground.

Table 4.3: Ratio of Community Nurses to Total Population and the 65+
Population

LHO Area	1	2	3	4	5	6	7	8
Ratio of Nurses to Total Pop.	1:2454	1:2627	1:2373	1:3204	1:3067	1:2162	1:2483	1:3195
Ratio of Nurses to over 65s	1:327	1:318	1:235	1:300	1:221	1:193	1:318	1:230

The disparity between LHOs in terms of the ratio of community nurses
to the older population is clearly demonstrated in Table 4.3 above. Area
6 has the highest levels of provision of community nurses both for its
older citizens and its total population. Area 4 has marginally the lowest
coverage in terms of its total population, but LHO one is least well
served in terms of its older population with only one community nurse
per 327 people over the age of 65.

The Generic Home Help Budget

It is important in this chapter to give an initial introduction to the home help service, because whilst non-profit organisations are *providers* of services, the *financing* for these is for the most part supplied and monitored by LHOs via section 65 grants. This role forms part of the duties of the managers of services for older people in each of the LHOs. In 1968, the *Care of the Aged* report (Inter-Departmental Committee on the Care of the Aged, 1968) argued for the establishment of a formal home help service in Ireland. Two years later this was officially enshrined in legislation under section 61 of the 1970 Health Act, which empowered but did not oblige the health boards to make arrangements for the provision of formal home care services. External bodies, such as the National Council for Ageing and Older People and the Policy Research Centre, have periodically evaluated the progress of this service delivery, both nationally and at the local level. Resulting recommendations have repeatedly advocated a range of improvements including enhanced pay, status, training and supervision of the home help service; optimisation of communication between the home help organisations and the health services; more efficient complaints procedures and national standardisation of assessment; and clearer criteria of entitlement and equitable provision. Many of these will be examined in the next chapter which explores the policy issues, organisation and practice of the home help service. This chapter contains a brief introduction to this purchaser-provider alliance between the state and the non-profit sector.

There are approximately one and a quarter million home help hours provided by 28 non-profit home help organisations across Dublin annually.[5] Our data also suggests that there is enormous variation between the numbers of home help hours currently being provided by the different LHO areas as demonstrated in Figure 4.3. There seems to be a clear but loose relationship between the number of home help organisations (Figure 4.2) and the number of home help hours provided so that the areas with the largest number of organisations also provide the largest number

---

[5] Three organisations normally categorised under area 2 are currently also working in area 3.

of hours, but the precise relationship between the number of organisations and the number of hours varies.

Figure 4.2: Number of Non-Profit Home Help Organisations per LHO in Dublin

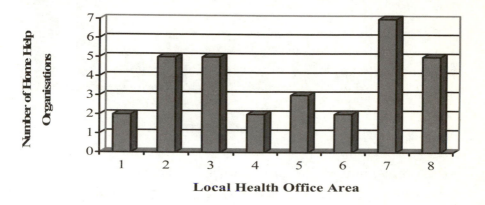

At first sight most striking is the difference between areas 1 and 7 with just under nine times the number of total home help hours funded by the latter LHO. Also notable is the large number of non-profit providers of home help in area 7 and the particularly large size of the organisations in area 8, based on the crude indicator of total hours of care provided divided by the number of organisations. Indeed if these calculations are worked out for each of the LHOs, this picture of unequal provision is further reinforced with organisations in north and west Dublin generally employing much larger numbers of workers than those in the south.

Figure 4.3: Number of Annual Home Help Hours Provided per LHO in Dublin

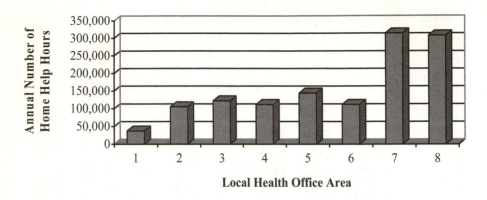

An interesting picture also emerges when the numbers of recipients of home help in each LHO are identified as in the following table.

Table 4.4: Home Help Recipients per LHO area

LHO Area	1	2	3	4	5	6	7	8
Average of +65 HH Recipients per Month	342	909	958	951	818	841	1505	2311
Recipients as % of Older Pop.	2.0	7.1	7.	7.0	9.0	5.7	9.3	13.0
Monthly Mean Average of Hours per Recipient	9.1	9.7	10.6	9.8	14.7	11.1	17.4	11.1

When the number of recipients is calculated as a percentage of the older population of the LHO, it can be seen that LHO area 1 again has significantly less provision than its sister areas. Area 6 also has quite a low rate of service provision, with less than 6 per cent of its population over 65 receiving home help hours. Using this very crude indicator, the older people in LHO 8 are by far the most likely to receive some form of home help service. The number of hours that an individual client receives is of course highly variable in practice, but it seems statistically probable that an older person living in either area 7 or 5 will have the opportunity to receive substantially more home help hours per month than in other locations around Dublin.

Interviewees were asked to provide figures on the numbers of total home help hours being supplied for older people in their LHO area, as well as the number of recipients in this age category. Some managers advised caution when examining the statistics as some home help organisations may simply provide a homogenous count of all categories of home help recipients, including older persons, families in distress, disabled persons, persons with psychiatric or intellectual difficulties and persons with hepatitis. Although the reports provided by the LHOs were of varying detail, all but one appeared to distinguish older persons as a category.[6]

In certain cases, the quality of data collection was good enough to allow internal comparison. For instance, in 2005 area 7 provided a total of 392,622 home help hours, of which 313,784 were allocated to older persons. This suggests that 80 per cent of all their home help hours are provided to older people. In contrast only 1,505 persons out of the 2,011 (75 per cent) actual recipients in the area were older persons. This is marginally lower than figures quoted in earlier reports such as Haslett, Ruddle and Hennessy (1998) and Finucane, Tieman and Moane (1993) who suggest that approximately 80 per cent of home help recipients nationally tend to be in this age category (i.e. 65 years or over). Some areas were slightly higher than this average such as LHO 5, where 82.46 per cent of the people assisted by the three home help organisations are older persons.[7]

In common with the findings above, Dramin (1983) identified inequities in resource distribution in a survey of home help services for older people in the Eastern Health Board area. Using returns from 1982 he argued that the percentage of older people in receipt of home service in (then) community care area VII was five times greater than in area I.

---

[6] The quality and extent of the formal data collection and reporting techniques fluctuates between LHO areas and organisations suggesting that the information provided should be treated only as an approximate indication.

[7] Considerable diversity exists even within this single area — the organisation that covers Inchicore reported 92.7 per cent of its clients as "aged" whilst the returns from the service that covers Clondalkin, Lucan and Rathcoole reported this category as constituting 72.2 per cent of client cohort.

This ratio continues today, though as noted in Figure 4.3 the differential is even greater if one uses the annual number of hours provided as the primary indicator, especially considering that their population sizes are roughly equivalent. This disparity persists to date, despite the fact that area 1 has a slightly higher percentage of older people at 13.34 per cent than area 7 at 12.8 per cent.

Why then, does this differential exist? Anecdotal evidence suggested by a range of interviewees suggests that there are fewer people likely to claim home help in area 1, perhaps due to the relatively high number of wealthy neighbourhoods. Noteworthy is the fact that a substantial number of private home care companies operate in this area. Some interviewees also suggested that there are problems recruiting sufficient numbers of home helps to provide a comprehensive service and levelled criticism at the ability of home care organisations in the area to successfully expand to the size required to effectively service the local population. It is also useful to note here that areas 1 and 2 have been involved in piloting the *Slan Abhaile* project enabling intensive and integrated care at home for a sample of older people being discharged from acute hospitals.[8] A sizable non-profit rehabilitation and home care company is the partner responsible for providing the care within this programme. At the time of interview, there were 28 recipients within the *Slan Abhaile* project. Area 1 is also piloting a scheme providing home-based care through a private care company. This initiative, propelled forward by problems recruiting health care assistants locally, is testing a detailed service level agreement. At the time of writing 14 clients had been accepted into the pilot exercise.[9] It is unsurprising that area 1, with its relatively small population of non-profit providers, health care assistants and home helps, should go down this route. Indeed, this area was also instrumental in the development of the home care grant scheme that is discussed in the next section.

---

[8] A similar project called *Home First* was also piloted in area 8.

[9] See Chapter Five for more detail on this.

Home Care Packages

In 2001, the Department of Health document *Quality and Fairness – A Health System for You* acknowledged that a large number of older people wanted the choice of receiving care at home rather than in a nursing home and recognised that current funding arrangements were not sufficient to successfully support home care. It was stated that the Government intended to make such financing a feasible option through the development of home care subvention schemes (Timonen, 2004). The need to redress the imbalance against home care was reinforced by the figures presented in the *Department of Social and Family Affairs Report* (2002) which pointed out that whilst expenditure between 1993 and 1996 on community services had only risen by 8 per cent, spending on the nursing home subvention scheme had amplified by 422 per cent within the same period of time.

The Health Boards were not obliged to follow the recommendation to put home care grant schemes into action at this time, but three initially stepped forward to launch pilot studies: the North Western, the Northern Area and the East Coast Area Health Boards. An evaluation of the latter two schemes was carried out by Timonen (2004) who observed that:

> In both health boards, the home care grants are intended to enable the purchasing of *additional* services i.e. the intention is to *complement*, not to replace health board services such as home help and public health nursing services. (Timonen, 2004, p. 5)

Aimed at removing or postponing the need for institutional care for older persons, it was intended that the grants be accessible both to those being discharged from hospital and those currently in the community to prevent them from having to go into hospital or long-term care.

By the end of the evaluation in 2003, 134 individuals in the East Coast Area Health Board had been approved for the home care grant whilst 58 people were in receipt in the Northern Area Health Board (Timonen, 2004). Table 4.5 shows the numbers of grants available approximately two years later within the eight LHO areas of this study.

Table 4.5: Provision of Home Care Grants, First Quarter of 2006

Pre-2005 Health Board	East Coast[10]		South Western			Northern		
LHO area	1	2	3	4	5	6	7	8
Home care packages	130	104	77	94	73	127	170	177

The above figures were provided by managers of the services for older people or home care grant coordinators in each of the LHOs in the first quarter of 2006. The figures given are approximate as they change on a daily basis. Area 4 for instance had 94 packages running, but an additional 40 being processed or awaiting a client to be discharged from hospital. Of these several may be refused by the client or not required should a nursing home option be chosen. The numbers thus collected in the table are based on grants currently in action at the time when the information was collected in early 2006. Provision of grants in the LHOs under the old Northern and East Coast Area Health Boards has continued to increase substantially. LHO areas 3, 4 and 5 are more recent participants in the scheme but are already beginning to process large numbers of applications.

An important distinction that the evaluation picked up between the schemes was that the East Coast Area Health Board made prospective payments directly to *recipients* allowing them complete freedom to choose their own providers of care, whereas the Northern Area Health Board paid the *provider* directly after the services had been rendered by one or more companies listed as "approved" by the Health Board (Timonen, 2004). This difference in systems endures partially into 2006 though some of the recommendations mentioned in the evaluation such as closer monitoring procedures have been implemented. Arguments made by managers in support of the idea of direct payments to recipients suggested that this method created more choice for both older people and their carers. One manager felt that "it would be disempowering to the client if the right to choice is removed". At the moment the recipient can

---

[10] The ECAHB also covered area 10 (Wicklow) which is not included in our study.

choose to allocate more money towards respite care than domestic help, or personal care, should they desire, they can also select any company or carer willing to meet their needs. Critics of the above method have asserted that it is open to abuse or can be confusing and time-consuming to some recipients who may be uncomfortable with managing it themselves. One manager, well acquainted with this possibility, was keen to point out that in cases like this they have procedures to provide other more suitable options if appropriate.

LHO areas 3, 4 and 5 as relative latecomers to the home care grant scheme initially decided to offer both options of direct payment to recipients or payment to providers, though recently it is being suggested in area 3 that they follow the Northern area model of funnelling the home care grants through designated private or non-profit care organisations. Area 5 is also planning to move to this system, as they found some clients were having trouble managing direct payments. One director of public health nursing wanted to make clear that her area will not give the grant directly to people who do not have their house insured to cover the home carer:

> Those clients who hire carers directly need to get employer's insurance in order to be covered. If the agency receives the money then this obviously is a different situation, though there actually is a question of whether all the private agencies are fully covered.

This latter point about insurance will be examined in detail in Chapter Six. Some managers in the LHOs in the old South Western Board also noted that because of the small size of the care agencies in their areas they are having difficulties recruiting fully insured companies with good staff training programmes to provide the care. One interviewee explained:

> We are chasing some of the larger private care agencies and trying to use those who have insurance and some form of training for their employees, but again no-one is checking up on them as such. The way it is going and we use one or two agencies, it will cost a lot and we'll have to go to tender and

> we'll have to draw up standards about how an agency inducts
> and trains its staff . . . the push has just been to discharge peo-
> ple from hospital . . . these things will have to come into play.

A manager of services for older persons in another LHO area argued that although they would ideally prefer to use non-profit organisations to deliver their home care grants and that the money would be available from the HSE, many of these organisations do not have the staff resources to meet the increased demand. This issue will be explored in following chapters, but it should be noted that managers in different areas have distinctly divergent experiences regarding the private/non-profit mix, with some preferring the former, others the latter or a combination of the two.

One manager stressed how "exciting" and "worthwhile" the current ambition of enabling older people to remain living in their own homes was. However, this interviewee was very aware of the "risk elements" associated with this ambition. At the moment, LHO areas are responsible for the delivery of state-funded domiciliary care, as they administer the home care packages. Most LHO managers suggested that they would be more comfortable with the home help organisations delivering the packages as they are "linked more closely" to the HSE structures. There is a non-profit organisation in area 8, for example, that has actively embraced the idea of home care grants and has restructured itself to provide this service on a large scale. There is also a large non-profit organisation, nominally based in area 2, to which several LHO areas have ties. Indeed, this organisation has sent a number of home helps for training to the personal carer level by the HSE. When asked why this company was used to deliver a large share of home care packages, interviewees responded that it has a "critical mass of resources" and acts in a "professional" manner. The contracts they issue to their staff were argued to be clearer and the procedures they have in place more transparent than in many other home help organisations and companies.

Some LHO areas, however, reported that a number of the home help organisations are struggling with the provision of the required numbers of home help hours under the generic budget, and are not interested in expanding their services to accommodate home care packages or the delivery of services outside normal working hours. Although some managers noted that they have concerns about many private sector companies, specific private companies were cited as informally preferred suppliers due to their cost, reliability, training or insurance status. Some managers also stated that the private sector is able to deliver a large number of hours in a more flexible manner and also able to speedily recruit additional care staff if required. One manager suggested that the commitment to agencies is shorter-term than the commitment to HSE employees. It is clear that in times of financial stress it would therefore be easier for the government to cut funding. Several managers of services for older people noted that they thought that more formal tendering procedures would be necessary in the future as cash flows to the private sector continue to expand.

Eligibility to the home care subvention scheme in all jurisdictions is based on means-testing, though one home care package coordinator asserted that this is changing:

> Requirements for getting the home care grant have been falling off as time has gone by. Originally you were allowed a certain amount in savings or pension; now savings or assets aren't taken into account at all unlike nursing home subvention. This is to speed up the process of getting people out of the hospitals as checking financial assets would take up considerable time as people didn't want to declare their savings. The limit was originally €8,000 and then this went up to €40,000, but most people don't know that. As time has gone by, and pressure to speed things up has built they have started to say savings aren't part of the assessment — the only thing that is taken into account is weekly income, which for most older people is a pension.

At the time of this interview in late 2005, weekly income was the primary category for financial assessment, though whether spousal income was taken into account remained to be clarified due to the rapid speed of procedural change. At another interview, it was argued that it is often difficult to manage the expectations and demands of families, and the suggestion was made that many families may be in a position to part-finance the care themselves. The debate over means-testing will be ex-

plored in more detail in subsequent chapters, but the perspective shared
amongst several of the managers of services for older people was that
equitable and clear guidelines to assessment and eligibility need to be
established. In terms of distribution, one manager advocated that fixed
amounts should be made available to persons based on their specific
level of dependency.

At present, most home care grants can only be secured through hospital discharge procedures. According to a number of managers of services for older people, the relative scarcity of home care grants available
from the community side was a real problem. For instance, it was argued
that the practice of prioritising hospital discharges had the unintended
consequence of *encouraging people to seek hospital admission*, to help
them secure a home care grant. This is further compounded by the fact
that the amount of money available through the hospital grant scheme is
considerably more than the community based alternative. The delayed
discharge initiative package for example will normally start at around
€350 a week, with grants of €500–600 available for higher dependency
cases. The community referred home care grants on the other hand are
limited to €190 per week. LHOs operating the *Home First* scheme have
slightly greater latitude for higher dependency cases, but the number of
packages available remains limited. Moreover, one interviewee noted
that they are only permitted to award one new community services-based
grant per month, but no ceilings are placed on hospital referred home
care grants which operate in cycles of 30 grants at a time.

Assessment and Review of Care Needs

Assessment and review of care needs is another area in which managers
believed that improvements could be made. Complaints were made by
several directors of public health nursing that people being discharged
from hospitals were being given an unrealistic picture of the levels of
help they could expect to receive once back at home. As one interviewee
put it:

> It seems to be that when people are in hospital they are given
> an incorrect perception of the services that are available in the
> community, by the acute hospitals. They have been told they

are going to get x, y and z and people think that the minute
they arrive out of hospital they are going to have a Rolls-
Royce service when they get home. And that isn't reality. This
is a difficulty we are trying to resolve.

Despite comments like these, some interviewees indicated that communications between community-based services and hospital-based professionals were starting to improve. Another interviewee emphatically
stated that one of the most serious gaps in provision of services for older
people in Ireland is the lack of community-based social workers dedicated to the *general* welfare of older persons. From the public health
nursing perspective, this means they are getting new clients with whom
they may have had no prior contact in the community, so they have to
rely on the assessments of individuals made in hospitals. One home care
package coordinator noted that in the case of home care packages there is
a discrepancy in assessment between the areas that process the grants
through a central interface (relying on the PHN body of staff for the assessment), and those areas that employ a dedicated case worker who
does both assessment and processing. One such case worker commented
that due to the expansion of the home care packages, they had been over-
loaded with so many cases that they are being forced to focus on processing money, rather than fully assessing and reviewing cases as intended. One suggested solution was to have PHNs take care of the lower
dependency community grants and employ case managers to monitor the
more complicated higher dependency packages.

Many interviewees believed that the current assessment process is
clearly inadequate and several stated that it is imperative to create "standardised assessment tools" that are nationally implemented for home
care packages. A director of public health nursing suggested that it is
important to measure activities of daily living (ADLs) which *also* include carer's needs, health and social needs, and mental health measure-
ments. This point was reinforced in a separate interview by a manager
who commented on the current lack of emphasis on social and companionship aspects in care packages for older persons. This manager asserted that whilst care packages for (younger) disabled persons often
make allowance for leisure activities and "quality time", this is not the

case for older persons who receive only the personal and household care that is deemed "necessary". Interviewees suggested that there is an opportunity here for organisations focused on providing companionship to cater for the social needs of older persons.

The lack of systematic review procedures in place for the packages was cited as a serious shortcoming. One manager noted that one of the key objectives is to help people develop or retain their independence in the community. Without a review after three months, some recipients start seeing their allocated level of care as a right, whereas this manager would hope that certain categories of client would improve and require less intensive levels of care. In this interviewee's opinion, a proper review system has the ability to reshape the care needed appropriately; the current system, it was argued, has the effect of making people more dependent rather than independent (although the opposite, situations where insufficient care is available, also clearly occurs and is very undesirable). LHO areas 6, 7 and 8 were at the time of the interviews collaborating on a project to develop review forms for the home care packages scheme. While this is a highly commendable endeavour, ideally such assessment and review protocols should be developed at the national level, i.e. through collaboration between all the LHOs in the country.

Despite the recommendations for improvements argued above, many managers felt that the introduction of home care packages had been of huge benefit, providing the means to enable more people to return to or remain at home. Referring to the enormous strain which is often placed on family carers, particularly spouses, one manager stressed that the advent of home care packages has ensured some relief for many family carers looking after persons with extensive care needs, especially when night-time care is provided to allow some respite. A public health nursing director concluded that whilst home care packages have been expanding, they are primarily a result of the need to "free up beds in hospital". This places a lot of extra pressure on PHNs in the community. This book therefore recommends further research to re-evaluate the staff ceilings and recruitment and retention measures currently in place for the community nursing staff within the LHOs in order to accommodate the increasing demand for their services. The following section discusses the role of the public sector in the direct provision of domiciliary care services outside the nursing profession.

The Role of the Health Care Assistant (HCA)

The position of health care assistant was introduced along with the District Care Units at the start of the 1990s, in part to ease the pressures on the public health nurses and as a result of a growing awareness that a different kind of (non-medical) care worker was needed to provide personal care. Originally attached to specific District Care Units, health care assistants have increasingly moved into more general non-medical community roles based out of health centres. While they are supervised and loosely monitored by the PHNs, most in the Dublin area are employed by Eastern Community Works[11] rather than directly by the HSE.[12] The public health nursing directors and health care assistants interviewed who had been with the service since its establishment suggested that this state of affairs had been intended to be temporary whilst they piloted the health care assistant, or "home care attendant" role as it was originally called. It remains a source of contention for many heath care assistants who feel that their enduring relationship with Eastern Community Works is reducing their status within the health service and means that they continue to be denied access to the HSE pension schemes.

As can be seen from Figure 4.4, the numbers of health care assistants in the community are very low and with recruitment problems and staff limits restricting their numbers for the last half decade, many directors complained that the demand for their services is outstripping supply. Areas 1, 2 and 5 all reported having at least two vacancies at the time of interview. According to the public health nursing directors in the LHOs, the majority of health care assistants work an average of 20 hours per week, though many workers suggested that they are regularly offered overtime. Some areas have a small number of full-time health care assis-

---

[11] Eastern Community Works (ECW) was set up in the 1980s to do jobs for older people such as minor repairs to their houses. The service is nowadays very limited as numbers of volunteers have dropped during the recent years of economic prosperity in Ireland.

[12] There were reports of a very small number of health care assistants directly employed by the HSE because they had transferred from hospital to community practice.

tants, though one director commented that she would not recruit on this basis again because of the irregularity of the hours and the physical stresses of the job.

Figure 4.4: Health Care Assistants (WTE) per LHO in Dublin

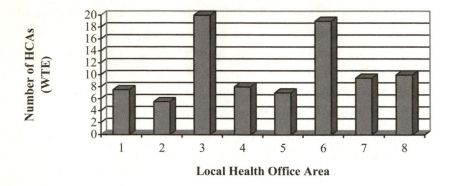

As Figure 4.5 shows, almost half the workers interviewed worked between 16 and 20 hours a week but none worked fewer hours than this. The times worked during the day vary, though many health care assistants operate between 9.00 a.m. and 1.00 p.m. They are often also expected to work weekend shifts on a rotating basis. Of all the LHOs in Dublin, only area 4 currently operates a twilight service. They have set up a rota system with their existing staff, and they visit the person seven days a week in the evening to provide assistance going to bed. Two of the assistants who work on the "back to bed scheme" were interviewed and noted that they each worked one evening a week from 4.45 p.m. for however long it takes them to complete their client visits. They are paid for four hours per evening regardless of the numbers of clients. This scheme has been in operation for 15 years. Generally both a health care assistant and a RGN conduct the visits together because of the dangers associated with evening calls. In the past LHO area 1 operated a similar service but it was discontinued several years ago. Several health care assistants thought the twilight service was in the process of being introduced in their areas.

Figure 4.5: *Number of Hours Worked per Week by Health Care Assistants Interviewed*

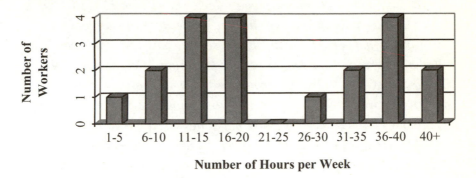

Number of Hours per Week

Vignette: Carol Nolan (name changed)

Carol is a health care assistant in her late 50s who has worked throughout north Dublin. She began working for the health board in the early 1990s, not long after the introduction of the "home care attendant" role. Carol prefers the new title as, "health is our primary responsibility and I don't want to be categorised as a home help, because I and my colleagues do a lot more than this in terms of how we help with mobility, the care of a patient's skin and how we work with and act as closer observer for the PHNs." Her pathway into caring began with volunteering; initially as a volunteer during school trips and then later for a major Irish disability association. It was here that she learned the basics of how to keep a patient clean. In the late 1980s a close family member was diagnosed with cancer and beyond some visits by the PHNs, there was very little support in the community. Carol nursed her relative until he died, at which point one of the visiting nurses asked her if she would consider applying for one of the new attendant positions. She started her new career working directly within a district care unit and still spends some time every week working for them despite the migration of most health care assistants to health centres and the general community teams. Carol works for around 25 hours a week in mornings, late afternoons and some weekends. She has approximately thirty clients, including four she sees on a daily basis and commented on the friendships she made in the job once she had gained the confidence of those she visited. Her years of experience have also taught her the importance of maintaining a professional persona, both with those she visits and in the eyes of the general public. The core of her training (like many health care assistants) revolves around a full-time five-week examined course, which she is later able to complement with refresher courses on manual lifting and handling, infectious diseases, etc. She gets a lot of satisfaction from being able to promote independence and dignity among her clients and especially likes helping people who are in low spirits to feel better. The worst aspects of her post include the amount of work that is increasingly being placed on health care assistants by the clinics and the inequitable pay levels between hospital health care assistants and those working in the community.

The work of community-based health care assistants is frequently very demanding. Often described by PHNs as "personal care", many workers stressed the varied and changing nature of their job. Standard tasks involve washing and dressing their clients, lifting, help with passive exercise if the occupational therapist or physiotherapist has left instructions. But they are not expected to get involved with the tasks judged to be in the province of the RGN such as changing catheters,[13] bowel care, medication administration etc. All 20 of the health care assistants involved in the study made clear they were not supposed to carry out any wound dressing, though several said they would fix dry dressings as a first aid emergency measure rather than leave a client in discomfort until the nurse visited. Beyond the standard routines of the work, however, the health care assistants considered an essential part of their role to act as a monitoring service for the nurses they worked with: assessing the physical condition, skin and abilities of their clients, and ensuring that they are coping and not suffering from any form of abuse. Another aspect of their

---

[13] There was some disagreement amongst health care assistants as to the limits of their responsibilities. One mentioned changing catheters, whilst others discussed the degree to which they would handle medication.

role often involves trying to help their clients through bereavement, or trying to get them through difficult times of the year such as Christmas. All agreed that there was an important social dimension to the job, of providing company to lonely and isolated clients, and some mentioned the pleasure that both they and the clients derived from simple tasks such as cutting hair or applying hand cream. Most suggested they would do a little cleaning or cooking for a client if it was required to make them comfortable, but all unanimously declared that they would not do home help type domestic work.

In contrast to workers within either the home help service or those working on home care packages, health care assistants in general tend to see a greater number of clients for a much shorter period of time on any given day. The following figure illustrates the number of clients per health care assistant per week. It illustrates that over two-thirds of the workers interviewed had between 16 and 25 clients. Notably none of our sample had less than ten clients.

Figure 4.6: Number of Clients per Health Care Assistant per Week

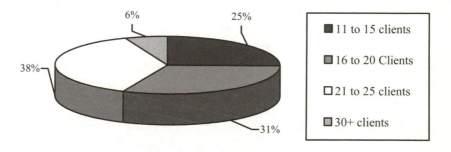

The length of time health care assistants spend with a client is not fixed and depends on the perceived needs of the client at any given moment, though a maximum of two hours was mentioned. Realistically this is not feasible in all but the most exceptional circumstances and several workers described the pressures of getting delayed during their schedule of visits. The average time most seemed to spend with a single client was 30-45 minutes, with the frequency of visits determined by dependency level and need. The district care units were set up to facilitate the rehabilitation of eligible people upon discharge from hospital. This is a short-term objective. The health care assistant position continues to play an important role in this objective, but many workers find that they are working with much longer-term clients now, often until death.

Another important component of the job is the time spent travelling between clients. This can be considerable for those working in rural areas where the clients are more spread out, or if the health care assistant has to travel across the LHO in busy traffic to reach the homes they need to visit. An oft-repeated wish was for the establishment of a system of parking permits because finding spaces for their cars in close proximity to their clients' houses is often difficult, frustrating and consumes time that could be better spent providing service. Most felt that they would rather not work in their own immediate neighbourhoods because of gossip and confidentiality issues. Workers get a banded travel allowance, plus a basic allowance of €10.00 a week for travel to and from their homes. There were some complaints that this allowance is seldom sufficient for their costs, especially during times of petrol price inflation. Those without cars are provided with a bus pass, though the availability of buses and bus routes is far from ideal for this type of work unless they are able to work with clients whose homes are clustered closely together.

Among the 20 health care assistants interviewed, there was considerable discord over whether they were satisfied with their rate of pay. Some felt that substantial improvements had been achieved, whereas others were under the impression that they were paid less than both their counterparts based in hospitals and home helps working for non-profit organisations. The latter was a particular source of irritation. Health care assistants are paid fortnightly and are on an incremental thirteen point scale, with €12.70 per hour as the highest rate available. There is a premium rate for Saturdays and double time is paid on Sundays. Compared to many carers working for non-profit or private companies, they have relatively good benefits attached to their job, such as 23 days holiday pay, up to five days uncertified sick pay, three months certified sick pay, and maternity leave. Several stated however that they are classified as temporary workers despite having worked more than four years in the service, and as noted they are not eligible for the HSE pension. For these reasons, as well as the increased status they feel it would bring, many argued very strongly that it is time for the HSE to recognise their contributions and employ them directly. Support for this idea could be found amongst some directors of Public Health Nursing and it was suggested that improved contracts are being negotiated alongside discussions with SIPTU, the trade union representing 18 out of the 20 health care assistants interviewed. Many of the workers, however, were sceptical that this would happen, with the majority believing that the union wasn't very interested in their plight because of their relatively small numbers.

LHOs 1, 2 and 7 all mentioned that they have found it difficult at times to recruit sufficient suitable staff to fill their allocation of health care assistants. Generally, the degree of turnover of HCA staff is very low. In our sample of 20, only three had been in the job for less than two years. Eleven of them had been working as assistants for between four and six years, whereas six had been employed since the early years of the creation of the position.

Figure 4.7: Length of Service amongst Employees

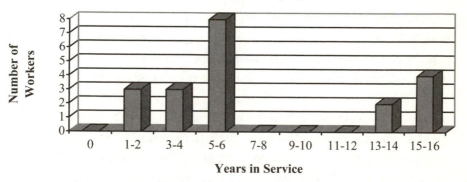

Interestingly, well over a third of interviewees were recruited by PHNs or other health care assistants, with the remainder responding to advertisements or applying off their own initiative. One had the post suggested to her by the home help organiser she was working for at the time. Each of the health care assistants interviewed were invited to discuss their various reasons for applying for the post; the reasons and the incidence of references are listed in Table 4.6.

Table 4.6: Reasons Given for Becoming a Health Care Assistant

Reasons	Incidence of References Made
Moved into it from previous formal care role	11
Independence from children going to school or leaving home	5
Moved into it after voluntary work in community organisations	4
Dissatisfaction with office/shop work	3
Flexibility of hours	2
Dislike of the heavy work in nursing homes	2
The experience of informal caring for a relative	2
Wanted a new challenge	2
Money needed so searched for a meaningful job	1

Workers described having generally good relationships with their clients, though a diverse range of positive and negative experiences were recorded from health care assistants because of the relatively large numbers of clients that they visit in comparison to a home help worker. Almost all health care assistants referred at some point in the interview to their love for the caring role and when asked about the best aspect of the work the most popular answer was the satisfaction derived from helping people regain their independence. Other statements included cheering people up, visiting the lonely, hearing and keeping people's secrets, feeling that they had made a difference and helping people pass away peacefully.

The large client base of the health care assistant suggests a propensity for substantially varying experiences in the relationship between carer and client. Some health care assistants were introduced to their new clients by the community nurses, but the majority noted that they have usually "gone in cold". Many alluded to the potential danger inherent in home visiting. A worker in a focus group described how she had recently been visiting a woman with dementia who refused to shower and who assaults her husband whenever he tries to clean her. She agreed to help the husband one day and experienced one of these attacks by the client when they tried to persuade her to shower. She noted that HCAs are not given the counselling training that may help them and the families to cope with such incidents.

Common reference was also made to the problems created by troublesome families. One assistant said that the part of the job she dislikes most is being perceived as the HSE representative and thus having to bear the brunt of the dissatisfactions of her more vocal clients and their families. Another assistant noted that she often gets very close to her clients, which makes it difficult to bear when she sees them being ignored or mistreated by their families. Another category of family member she is uncomfortable with are those who treat the client as if they are incapable of independent thought, insisting on answering everything for them. A number of carers expressed how they have to avoid getting involved in family arguments: "You become like family with many of the clients, and you can sometimes get people trying to drag you into blazing family rows! They'll ask you for your opinions."

In one focus group, the complaint was made that the PHNs to whom the HCA report are so busy that there is rarely anyone with whom they can debrief following these difficult occasions. The group made the suggestion that they would like to see the creation of a HCA manager post; someone recruited from their own ranks that appreciates and understands the work they do. This would also help towards the creation of an internal career pathway among health care assistants whilst adding a focused and central point for monitoring both the performance and wellbeing of often isolated health care assistants. Others suggested that it would be good to have access to bereavement counselling when they lose clients they are close to, or have more training in communications or in dealing with confrontational situations. Some suggested that the HSE should provide mobile phones or phone credits to health care assistants to facilitate their work.

The majority of health care assistants had experience in caring prior to their employment with the HSE. As reflected in Table 4.7, only five out of the 20 interviewed had no experience whereas eleven had previously done paid work in a caring or nursing occupation and four had experience as unpaid or volunteer carers.

Table 4.7: Previous Care Experience of Workers

Type of Experience	Numbers of Workers
None	5
Unpaid family carer	1
Unpaid neighbour/friend carer	1
Nursing home work	4
Private care agency work	1
Nursing experience	2
Non-profit home help	3
Voluntary associations with care aspect	2
Non-medical hospital work	1
Total	*20*

Health care assistants were generally amongst the most comprehensively trained carers in the non-medical community care arena. All are required to have completed manual handling and first aid courses, and many have also had additional training as part of established LHO training programmes (e.g. being sent to train at St Mary's in the Phoenix Park for several weeks) or via former employment in hospitals, nursing homes or home care companies. LHO 8 also holds an educational hour for its assistants once a month. Health care assistants throughout Dublin also gain direct informal experience when working with community nurses. One carer expressed frustration with some of the more informal training mechanisms she has encountered:

> Once I was asked if I wanted to go and hear a lecture on infectious diseases. I agreed and then when I got back I was told to give the lecture to my colleagues . . .

In recent years, the eight-module FETAC course has become the main source of formal training for HCAs. This is an intensive five-week course, sometimes undertaken on release from work over the course of a year. Each LHO is attempting to gradually cycle their workforce of assistants through this programme. Interviewees thought that there were only two course places per LHO area available per year. Over half of the assistants interviewed had completed this training with others hoping to do it. Generally speaking most were proud of this training and felt that it helped them understand their role better, though complaints were made that certain aspects of the FETAC course such as health and safety were focused on hospital-based workers rather than those working in the community. One noted that, "the course tutors are idealistic in their expectations of how much time we can spend with clients". Some interviewees felt that the effort put into this level of training should be rewarded with better pay and status.

A recurrent theme in the interviews was the discussion over whether or not the role of the health care assistants could be expanded via appropriate training to include jobs such as dry wound dressing in order to relieve some of the pressure from the community nurses. Many were quite interested in this idea though reservations were made about the responsibility and time commitment it might require. One public health nursing director discussing this option suggested that an evaluation would be needed to see what areas would be suitable for health care assistants to be "upskilled" in. This would include regular reports to the nurse about what they are doing as a stricter monitoring system would have to be developed than that which is currently in place. In her opinion, clear boundaries would need to be set so everyone felt competent and confident. It was also asserted that discussions about the introduction of different grades of health care assistant have been taking place within the HSE for several years, with opponents to the idea stating that implementing specialised training and payment grades may disrupt continuity of care by further widening the array of people going into a client's home. Several assistants mentioned that they would like further training, particularly when they have clients with specific illnesses or difficulties. Others mentioned that they would like some counselling training because of the number of social problems they witness, whilst some suggested that practical training such as how to cut hair would be very beneficial.

There was an assumption among some HSE managers that employment as a health care assistant can provide a step towards considerable "upskilling", especially if it is used as a route into nursing. Of the workers we interviewed, many felt too old for this or that the length of training time would dissuade them from this career pathway. Some had heard of other carers becoming nurses, and regretted that this was not an option for the majority because of difficulties of securing sponsorship.

Conclusions

This chapter has reviewed some of the key dimensions surrounding both the direct provision of community-based care services (PHN, HCA) and the financing and support by the State of non-profit and private providers of home care for older people in Dublin. Perhaps the most striking theme to emerge from the data is the uneven distribution of services (direct provision and especially indirect provision through the home help organisations) around the city.

From the perspective of directors of public health nursing, increases in the population of older persons, the changing focus towards community (rather than nursing home) care, coupled with HSE staff ceilings and nursing shortages, are creating a situation where they are unable to provide the level of service desired. The ambition of a community nursing service focused on prevention remains illusive 10 years after renewed calls for such improvements. Re-evaluating the existing staff ceilings may alleviate this pressure somewhat, but the problem of recruiting sufficient numbers of both nurses and health care assistants remains. It has been suggested that some of the workload on community nurses could theoretically be lightened by expanding the training and the role of the health care assistants to include some of the more routine duties of the nursing staff. This would require training and monitoring, but it should be noted that the idea was met with mixed reactions by both health care assistants and managerial staff. It was apparent that before such a move could even be considered, there would finally have to be a commitment by the HSE to directly employ the community-based health care assistants to achieve parity with their hospital-based counterparts.

Also observed in this chapter was the rapid development of the home care grant scheme over the last two years. The discussion about whether payments should be made directly to clients or to the service providers has not yet been conclusively resolved, though a gradual move towards the latter system seems to be emerging. There is also ongoing debate about whether it is preferable to utilise the existing non-profit organisations or develop the private sector as a means of servicing the packages. The consensus seemed to be that whilst many managers would ideally opt for the non-profit organisations because of the relationships already in place, apart from a few exceptions this was unlikely to happen because of the speed and degree of change needed. Many interviewees had reservations about a number of the private care companies however and it was suggested that a competitive tendering process needs to be implemented that outlines a requirement for clear standards concerning cost, reliability, training and insurance. National standardisation of assessment and review procedures were recommended as was the development of clear, well-publicised criteria for eligibility. If the community nursing body is to be central in such improvements, a full re-evaluation of current staff levels will be required to facilitate this. Some managers suggested that the establishment of a substantial system of community social workers would be a feasible solution to this predicament. Another important problem beginning to surface as the home care package scheme expands is the discrepancy between the numbers and value of packages that can be granted by the community care services in comparison to the hospital-based delayed discharge initiatives. Currently the unintentional situation exists where hospital admission is almost a prerequisite for older people to gain access to the home care package, thus exacerbating the larger problem of hospital crowding. Greater numbers of community-awarded grants, combined with an increase in the amount of money they provide, should help to reverse this ironic state of affairs.

Chapter 5

NON-PROFIT SECTOR: ROLE IN THE PROVISION OF HOME CARE

David Prendergast

Chapter 4 outlined the role of the HSE in the financing and direct provision of home care in Dublin. It explored the limits of direct provision from public providers such as health care assistants and community nurses, the impact of recent developments such as home care packages and established that, by far, the greatest numbers of paid home care hours are delivered by workers from the non-profit organisations. This chapter will examine the role of the non-profit home help organisations and their workers in the light of recent changes and challenges to the service.

Models of Home Help Organisations in Ireland

Following the legislative push to formalise the home care service at the start of the 1970s, a circular (11/72) was passed around the health boards from the Department of Health in April 1972 pressing for a voluntary rather than a statutory home help model. It stated:

> Only when it has been established without question that services of voluntary agencies cannot be utilised in the provision of the service should Home Helps be directly employed by the Health Boards. (Dept. of Health, 1972, point 7) (Quoted in Lundstrom and McKeown, 1994, p. 131)

Almost 35 years later, no single cohesive delivery model exists within Ireland. In 1994, Lundstrom and McKeown identified six basic service delivery models, four statutory and two voluntary, with great variation in the organisational links and complexity between the home help service and the public health nursing service. Only Dublin, north Tipperary, Clare and parts of Wicklow and Donegal, they argued, adopted a model where "voluntary bodies take responsibility for delivering the Home Help service . . . employ(ing) Home Help Organisers and Home Helps" (p. 129). They identified the following model operating in Dublin:

Figure 5.1: Model of Home Help Organisations in Dublin in 1994

The non-profit organisations are legally independent entities, financed by the HSE under section 65 of the Health Act 1953 which empowers the HSE to cover the costs of care, beyond the contributions made by the client when appropriate. Under this system, each organisation can claim the equivalent of the cost of a home help organiser for every 150 clients they have. Writing in 1994, Lundstrom and McKeown argued that the benefits of this system from the perspective of the health boards included voluntary organisations having local knowledge, contacts, involvement, support and goodwill; promoting a volunteer ethos; flexibility not possible within the health board; and a cheaper service. Unlike many areas outside Dublin where the public health nursing team has a much greater supervisory role in the home help service, the non-profit organisations were seen as autonomous, receiving referrals from PHNs but ultimately accountable to their committees rather than the health service.[1] This said, in practice, the non-profit home help organisations in Dublin are loosely monitored via a monthly or quarterly return-form which specifies the numbers of home helps employed, number of care hours provided and the number of clients. Additionally health professionals sit on many of the committees of the organisations.

Profiles of the Organisations

Many of the home help organisations in Dublin were formed in the early to mid-1970s. The two oldest organisations we interviewed were established in the late 1960s, around the time of the publication of *The Care of the Aged* report (Inter-Departmental Committee on the Care of the Aged, 1968) and just prior to the landmark Health Act 1970. Fourteen of the 19 Dublin organisations who participated in the study were originally set up by religious organisations, most notably the Little Sisters of the Assumption, though groups such as the Sisters of the Poor and Daughters of Charity were also heavily invested in the home help arena, as were some local clergy who set up their own initiatives. The Little Sisters of the Assumption started out working with ill or incapacitated mothers living in poverty, with older people initially a more marginal or subsidiary client group. The Order originally combined home help with home nursing, however once the public health nursing system was installed in the early 1980s, they were forbidden from offering a home nursing service and consequently began to focus explicitly on home help. The remaining organisations were created from neighbourhood volunteer groups or through the encouragement of the health authorities.

---

[1] There is just one non-profit home care organisation in Dublin that is an exception to this. This organisation has a home care organiser who is a direct employee of the HSE.

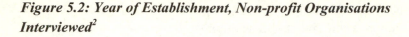

Figure 5.2: Year of Establishment, Non-profit Organisations Interviewed[2]

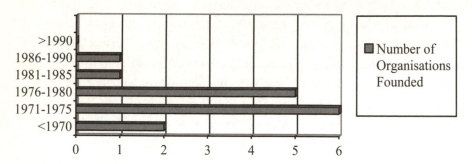

Thirty years later, very few of the home help organisations are directly run by religious groups, though several continue to retain clergy or nuns on their boards and management committees. In the majority of cases, however, the generation of nuns who were most active in the running of the home help service have either retired, handed over the management to lay committees and organisers, or felt that the formalisation of the service via changes in the laws surrounding taxation and employment of home care workers had moved the service away from its charitable volunteer roots. As explained by one organiser:

> . . . another reason the nuns wanted out of the home help business was because of the changes in PAYE rules. Treating home helps legally and financially as employees became too complicated for them. Sister Mona set it up as a young nun riding around on her bicycle encouraging neighbours to help. It grew so much that when she retired the nuns finally decided that they were doing the work of the health board and it had transcended charity.

The change in the employment laws in 2000 regarding home helps was arguably one of the defining moments in the evolution of the non-profit home care service. It has forced many organisations to perceive and treat

---

[2] Four of the 19 organisers interviewed were unclear about the origins of their organisation.

their home help workers as employees with social security rights rather than as volunteers. From the workers' perspective, the necessity of moving from an informal and flexible arrangement to becoming a tax-registered employee was sometimes unwelcome, especially if it was perceived as affecting welfare benefits. In the short term, it contributed to a large number of experienced home care workers leaving the occupation. Currently, however, the majority of the home helps appear satisfied with the overall improvement in their terms and conditions, although much room for improvement remains, as will be discussed later in this chapter.

Limited Company Status

Another consequence of this formalisation and the management shift away from religious institutions was that some home help organisations began to re-evaluate their own legal status and the personal liability of their board members. For some organisations, the forced transition to the legal role of employer signalled to their committees the necessity of establishing themselves as limited companies. For others, as in the former Northern Area Health Board, the home help organisations received information and recommendations from the HSE that they should seriously consider this option. A focus group of organisers from this region revealed mixed reactions to this recommendation. One board of directors believed that becoming a company would stabilise the organisation following the 2000 upheavals, however as one home help organiser put it:

> . . . now we are not so sure, as company law holds us in a strict set of procedures and we are now considering if there are alternative models out there that would be better suited for non-profit making organisations.

Fifteen out of the 19 non-profit home help organisations interviewed have become limited companies, and indeed several have held this status since as long ago as 1990. Many are satisfied with the situation, suggesting that it was a sensible move "in today's compensation society" or that the limited company documentation had "woken them up" to the pitfalls of mismanagement now that they handle such large sums of money. Disquiet was expressed, however, about whether this was another step away from the compassion, flexibility and altruism that had originally characterised the voluntary home help service. Others voiced deep suspicion about the motives of the HSE and questioned whether it was a clandestine effort to distance themselves from the home help organisations, as can be seen in the following quote from an organiser in north Dublin:

> There was an audit of an organisation in area eight, which revealed that it wasn't being run as efficiently as it could be . . . some serious accountancy mistakes . . . recommendation was that home help organisations should become liable as limited companies. The HSE would no longer have direct responsibility for mistakes made. All they would need to do is agree to a budget and stick to it. The problem is, if you do this, it's hard to get people to come forward and become company directors.

Another organiser claimed that her committee was composed of powerful community figures that refused to change the organisation to a limited company status, not least because of the extra bureaucracy, administration and legal responsibility they believed the transition would have entailed. Neither were certain organisers, who had made the change, always convinced that limited company status offered as much protection as they would like:

> What might a Leas Cross level incident amongst home helps from my organisation mean for our directors? We have a director who is a barrister who doesn't think we will be protected.

All of the Dublin-based non-profit home help organisations are legally independent from the HSE that acts to finance rather than directly provide home help. However, criticisms of interference by the health authorities in their business were levied by many organisers, particularly in relation to worries over what the approaching implementation of Service Level Agreements (SLA) will mean for them. Considerable consternation and confusion over these documents was evident. One organiser claimed that various organisations had received and compared SLAs and noticed subtle but important differences in them. Another claimed that the agreement she had seen had indicated that her organisation would receive a retrospectively paid rather than front-loaded budget. To this end, some organisers believed that they were being "steam-rolled" by a health authority attempting to introduce SLAs without proper consultation. One organiser noting that organisations who do not agree to the SLA could easily be "rolled up" by the HSE, asked who would pay for the redundancies of the care staff in this situation.

The "Organiser" Role

Opinion between organisers was divided about the overall benefits of being directly employed by the HSE. Whilst many felt that they would welcome the personal benefits involved (such as removal of the current cap on their salary, access to the HSE pension scheme, etc.), this would be counterbalanced by a growth in bureaucracy and corresponding loss of autonomy and flexibility that would compromise the home help service. The discussion in one focus group for a time revolved around the subject of whether the future would see the numerous small non-profit home help organisations subsumed into a few large organisations. It was semi-humorously commented that the health board is waiting for many of the older organisers to retire to achieve this objective. Other organisers suggested that good committees would simply hire replacements to ensure that this would not happen and argued that they are proud of what they have built up and would fight to see it continue. One practical reason for remaining independent is that organisers are currently able to continue working well beyond the retirement age required of HSE employees.

When asked to reflect upon their job roles, there was little disagreement that the pressure upon organisers had increased in recent years with administration duties taking up more time, especially since they had become responsible for managing the tax and PRSI of their staff. Several felt that the title "home help organiser"[3] did not adequately reflect their extensive managerial responsibilities as is evident from the following quote:

---

[3] The title "organiser" has been used in this study both because of its historical usage and the clarity of definition it provides when distinguishing between several occupations with similar job titles. We accept, however, the argument that the title "home care manager" is legitimate given the workload involved.

I would consider myself a "home care manager". The title "organiser" goes back many years but I have almost one hundred and fifty staff and nearly five hundred clients. I run what would be considered a medium-sized company. I want to be called a manager. If you compare us with organisations in the West for example, they work directly for the HSE and so have access to payroll departments, etc. We do that all ourselves. Our job is very detailed, very involved . . .

Another organiser listed some of the diverse duties expected in her post:

I come in the morning and check the calls, review our financial situation, interview home helps, bring in home helps for appraisal, do training, conduct assessment calls or reviews, not to mention supervisory calls on the home helps, attend case conferences and meet with relatives . . . I most enjoy meeting with the clients and being able to help them both practically and psychologically to stay in their homes in dignity. Conversely, not being able to meet their needs because of lack of personnel with the specific skills needed or budgetary constraints is the most frustrating part of the job.

Others added roles to this catalogue such as counsellor, social worker, book-keeper and home help on occasions when there is no-one available to fill in. The salaries of organisers are currently benchmarked and capped at a junior management level (level five) on the scales used by the HSE. All of them felt that this was inadequate considering the extent of their duties and responsibilities, particularly in light of the extra paperwork that is now being created by the influx of home care packages. Some described the stress of regularly working through weekends and evenings and how an increased administration load is reducing the time they have available to visit and review their clients. This latter complaint was expressed by several of the organisers, as was frustration with budgetary cuts such as those experienced in 2005 leaving some organisations over-committed and under-funded.

Home Care Packages

The provision of home care packages by the non-profit home help organisations around Dublin has been inconsistent. In the main, private agencies provide the carers to meet the expanding demand being created by the new packages in both the former East Coast Area and South Western Health Boards. At the time of the interviews, four out of the ten non-profit organisations from these two regions participating in our study had not yet worked on a package, whilst the remainder had begun to take on only small numbers. In contrast, the non-profit organisations interviewed from the former Northern Health Board generally had a much greater rate of participation in the new home care packages scheme. Though several dealt with less than 20 packages, others had fully recognised the potential of this income stream and had restructured their businesses accordingly. One non-profit organisation in LHO area 8 for example provides a total of 156 home care packages, including nine 24/7 packages. This now accounts for 65–70 per cent of the total income of this organisation.

This latter organisation argued that by covering all the hours and times required by the individual packages they were able to ensure continuity of care. They also voiced reluctance to work with private agencies who might not be properly insured. Eight out of the 19 organisations stated that they were unable to provide care outside the hours 8.00 a.m. to 6.00 p.m. or at weekends, though some expressed a wish to do so. As one organiser put it, "we need to start thinking about older persons not ceasing to exist on Friday evening". Another home help organiser argued that she would like to make the service more widely available, especially at weekends, but that funding was simply not there; consequently the hiring of administrative and supervisory staff would have to come out of the generic home help budget. Several non-profit organisations compromise by providing care during the day for individuals on packages, with night or weekend work provided by private companies.

Reactions in general to the home care packages were very mixed among organisers. The organisation above that re-adapted itself as an active 24-hour provider operates within a health board area that chose to pay the provider directly rather than the home care recipient. In the former South Western Health Board area, which is currently experimenting with both funding methods, many concerns were outlined about the home care packages by one of its resident non-profit organisations. This organiser felt that the problems with direct payment include lack of accountability, potential for misuse by clients, and the fact that carers hired in this way do not always pay tax or PRSI. On the other hand, she also felt that the routing of care package monies to home help organisations was unnecessarily complicated:

> It's a method of taking over from the home help organisations . . . a separate stream of money . . . there are already too many separate streams of money.

The desire to see home care package funding channelled directly into the organisation like the generic budget rather than via the currently labour-intensive invoicing system was also voiced by one organiser who provides a substantial number of home care packages. This organiser stressed that she would like to see each package paid at a standard fee every month until circumstances change such as the person moves to a hospital or their needs alter. This would avoid the cash flow difficulties that some organisations are beginning to face as the numbers of home care packages increase. At the moment, they sometimes have to wait three months for the invoices to be paid. This was sustainable when the numbers of recipients was small, but with the rapid expansion of the scheme such delays can become financially problematic. Other concerns expressed included worry over whether the implementation of the home care package system was gradually being used to replace the generic home care budget and apprehension at whether they and their staff have the expertise and training to provide care to some of the highest dependency clients referred through the home care package scheme.

Voluntary Financial Contributions

One organiser from north Dublin pointed out that home care package recipients are not obliged to make a financial contribution towards the cost of care received. She argued that this is creating a two-tier system which may cause problems in the foreseeable future. As noted earlier, voluntary contributions by clients towards the cost of home help have been encouraged from the inception of many of these organisations. This policy remains in place in the majority of the organisations interviewed. Two companies didn't provide information on this subject, but of the remaining 17, 11 collect contributions.

*Figure 5.3: **Number of Organisations Requesting Voluntary Contributions***

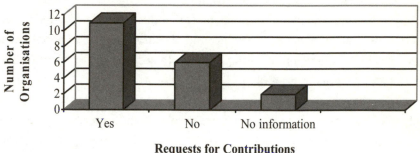

The amounts varied between organisations and clients, with some requesting as little as €3.00 per week; others on the other hand suggest the payment of the full cost of care if they believe a client can afford it. The following figure is derived from data provided by the organisations about what levels of contributions they would request from clients who could afford it.

*Figure 5.4: **Approximate Contributions Requested from Clients***

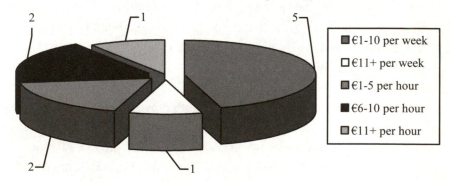

Some of the organisers request flat rates from their clients, others decide the level of contribution when doing the initial client assessment, whilst one suggested that she simply sits down with new clients, outlines the costs of care and negotiates with them what contribution they would like to make. All noted that certain clients such as the terminally ill or those living in poverty would never be required to pay voluntary contributions and that many refuse anyway. Collection methods ranged from sending monthly envelopes to their clients to having home helps collect it.

The reasons given by organisers for collecting contributions were numerous, but tended to cluster around the argument that people who pay tend to be appreciative of the home help service and are more likely to request a reduction in their hours if they improve. A perspective voiced by several home help organisers and HSE personnel was that this helps counter unrealistic expectations among some older people. It was argued that this was demonstrated, for example, by the number of cleaners who were sacked in anticipation of saving some money the *perceived* universalisation of home help with the introduction of the Medical Card for all aged 70 or over in 2001. One interviewee noted that her organisation did not ask for contributions until three years ago, but they were eventually forced to adopt this practice in order to make up for the shortfalls in their budgets and funding instability by the HSE. The amounts gathered via contributions vary greatly between organisations with some collecting enough for "petty cash" in which to buy the basics such as sheets and clothes for needy clients, whilst others noted they collect and report to the HSE amounts as large as €7,000 per month or roughly 20–25 per cent of their expenditure. These latter organisations believed that this contribution was deducted from their generic budget, though one said that she uses the money to subsidise a meals-on-wheels service affiliated to her organisation.

Of those that do collect contributions some felt that this was a worthy practice whilst others clearly felt discomforted by it. One organiser noted that it can cause problems because "some don't ask for contributions" and "everyone seems to know someone who isn't paying as much as they are". Explanations given by the six non-profit organisations who did not ask for contributions included the belief that services should be free to those in old age or that assessing people for contributions was "just too messy" and complicated. An interviewee argued that some older clients might turn down the service or not seek it if charges were involved, which she felt would be most unfortunate. She went on to say that forgetfulness on the part of some clients would also be a problem; if payment is up to such clients, it is not fair to the care workers, particularly if the contribution forms part of their direct income. Another organisation used to collect, but stopped on the orders from their committee who were advised that this could lead to questions of accountability.

Client Composition

As Figure 5.5 below shows there was considerable diversity in the size of the non-profit organisations interviewed. More than two thirds (n=11) had less than 300 clients. There were five with between 400 and 500 clients, but only one with a very large client base of 910 recipients at the time of interview.

Figure 5.5: The Size of Non-profit Home Care Organisations Interviewed

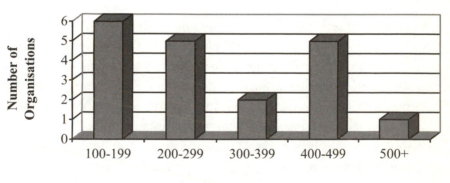

The following chart, drawn from the impressions of the organisers, shows that older people remain the primary focus of these organisations, though interestingly two organisations reported fewer than 70 per cent of their client base as being aged 65+. These were located in expanding areas towards the city boundaries where a great deal of new housing is be-

ing built and the population as a whole is generally younger. These organisations reported high numbers of clients belonging to groups named
as families in stress, disabled, hepatitis sufferers or people with mental
health problems.

***Figure 5.6: Percentage of Activity Focused on Clients Aged 65+ by
Organisation***

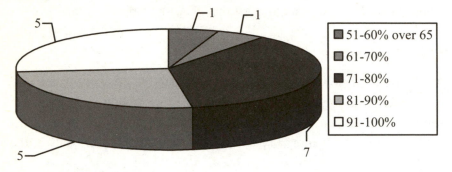

Referrals

A manager of services for older people in Dublin noted that the current
health service is "reactive crisis-driven" rather than "preventive proactive", which would make it unsurprising that all the organisers we interviewed pointed towards hospital social workers as the primary source for
clients, with many suggesting that this avenue provides as much as 60
per cent of their referrals. Community services and Public Health Nurses
(PHNs) were the second most frequent source of referrals with the remainder coming from GPs, community and voluntary organisations,
clergy, family members and self-referrals. Community social workers
were also on this list, but mainly for cases concerning families in distress. Waiting lists were common for clients judged to have lower dependency needs, especially in areas where the supply of home care
workers is limited or at times of high demand.

Assessment

Because of the independent nature of the home care organisations in Dublin, control over the assessment of client need and subsequent allocation of hours is the carefully guarded responsibility of the home help organisers. The HSE provide the financing for a general budget of home care hours but it is the organisers' duty to decide exactly how those hours will be distributed among their clients.

A typical scenario would involve the home help organiser receiving a referral from a gatekeeper such as the PHN who will have done their own assessment on the nursing needs of the client and will often recommend the number of home help hours that are needed. Complaints were levied about the lack of medical information the organisers are sometimes given, particularly if they are kept in the dark about a psychiatric condition. Some organisers expressed irritation at nurses, GPs or social workers who either attempt to dictate the number of home help hours needed or over-inflate the expectations of the clients. As one interviewee explained to the general amusement of her colleagues in the focus group, "the nurse just recommends the level of hours needed. They learn the hard way." She went on to say that whilst most PHNs have got used to the fact that the decision lies with the organiser and that this practice is backed by the unions, this is something that often has to be taught to new nurses. Another in the same group commented that she found GPs to be unrealistic in their expectations of the amount of help a client might actually need and what the service can realistically provide.

Upon receiving a referral, most organisers will arrange to visit the client in their home where they will sit down and chat to the client, observe the home and social situation and investigate what chores they require and what the client feels they would have difficulty doing. One explained that beyond an inspection of the accommodation, this involves assessing personal needs such as nutrition, heating, environment, social needs and the degree to which family and neighbours may wish to be included in the cycle of care. This can unleash a multitude of fragile emotions and family politics, with some family carers feeling threatened or guilty. For this reason the interview must be approached with the utmost sensitivity:

> No-one taught us to do the assessments. No apathy has set in
> amongst us. We don't go in with preconceived ideas or some
> kind of storyline from professionals such as PHNs — usually
> we won't get a copy of their assessments. I hate to say this, but
> out of fourteen referrals from PHNs, seven will end up in re-
> fusals. People need convincing to take the service.

This latter point is important. For some clients, the idea of having a
stranger in their house is not a comfortable one. For others, it signals a
decline into dependency. This provides an interesting contrast to those
clients with expectations that the organisers feel are impractical. One
wryly noted that she assesses them for their "needs rather than wants"
and several pointed out that they have to constantly explain that they are
not a cleaning service and most certainly "don't do silver".

Like many managers and directors in the community care service, a
number of the organisers complained about unrealistic expectations created during the hospital discharge procedure:

> People don't often need hospital level services at home, and
> the hospitals seldom know the true picture of what's going on
> in the home or the help to be got from neighbours, etc. Ap-
> proximately a third of the referrals I get from hospitals are for
> people who don't even want it once they are in their own
> homes.

Another noted:

> When people are discharged we often get family members
> who will quote a nurse who said mum would need twenty-four
> hour care. This will stick in their heads more than what is ac-
> tually being said at the case conference. Consequently organ-
> isers have to often gently explain that twenty-four hour care
> would certainly not be a community resource. Social workers
> are getting better at this. The problems arise in terms of hours
> allocated when people begin to compare with their neighbours
> and get jealous.

Workforce Profile

This next section outlines the composition of the workforce employed by the non-profit home care organisations. Before exploring the perspectives of the workers delivering the care, facets of the non-profit domiciliary sector are first reviewed including the numbers of carers employed, recruitment and remuneration of care staff, as well as training and monitoring procedures employed.

Composition of the Non-profit Care Workforce

Of the 19 organisations interviewed, 11 had between 50 and 100 care workers. Only one had more than 200 workers on their books. The vast majority of these workers were part-time and most were reported as primarily working in a domestic work rather than personal care role. However, several estimated that between a quarter and a third of their workers operated in both roles, i.e. they deliver both personal care and home help. Only two reported the majority of their workers as working in a dual capacity and one of these was the large organisation that has been actively restructuring itself to cater for home care packages.

Figure 5.7: Number of Workers per Organisation Interviewed

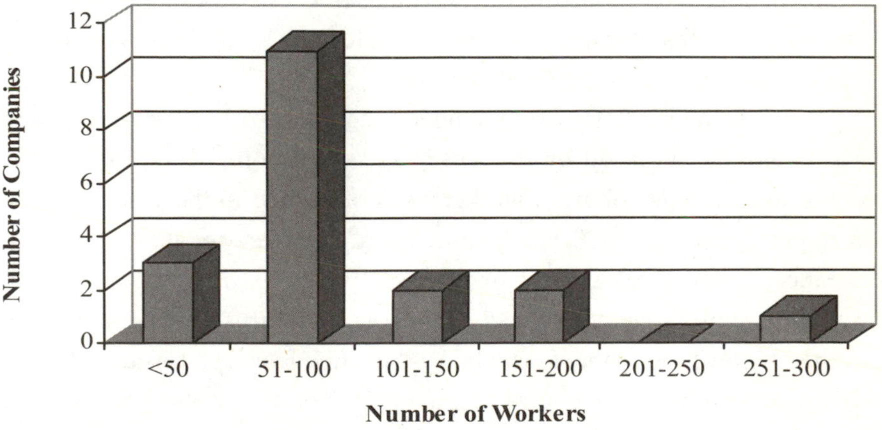

The care workforce in Dublin's non-profit organisations is almost entirely female with only seven of the 19 companies employing men. Of these seven organisations, most employed just one or two males, usually for specialist roles or clients; one organisation (which was an exception) hired four men. Similarly, only very small numbers of non-Irish staff were employed in the non-profit organisations. Many claimed that this was due to lack of applications, work permits, or the necessity of requiring a high level of English language competency when working with older people. Only two of the organisations interviewed employed more than ten non-Irish workers. One of these organisers suggested that even within the boundaries of her specific area, certain communities were more accepting of non-Irish workers than others.

The age range of home helps is very diverse with ages varying between 18 and 80 years though most organisations indicated that the majority of their workers are aged between 30 and 55. Seven of the organisations also pointed out that they have home helps working into their 70s. Most felt that older carers tend to manage well, and statements emerged such as "these are the ones who will often go far beyond the basics to cater for the needs of the client" or "we need older carers because some clients request someone closer to their own age. Older carers don't rush around as much, for example picking kids up from school and so have a bit more time on their hands." One organiser said that she had a few older carers working for her, but that she would hesitate to actively recruit anyone over 65 because health and safety is becoming such a central issue, and that she didn't think she could "ask a 65- to 70-year-old to carry a hoover up two flights of stairs".

Some believed that a new younger generation of home care workers was emerging, attracted by the wages and conditions of the job. It was suggested that this cohort of workers was interested in the work because at approximately €13.00 per hour it pays considerably more than, for instance, contract cleaning work, which typically pays the minimum wage. Organisers were not overly concerned with this new development as they believed only those who had a "genuine leaning" towards the job would remain in the long term because of the nature of the job, the hard work it entailed and the uncertain hours.

Categories of workers identified by organisers included mothers whose children had started school or left home, people who have cared for family members who then decided they wished to carry on in the care role, or women who had separated from their husbands and needed a flexible job that could fit around their childcare needs. One organiser took some pains to note how important home care employment is in some economically deprived parts of the city.

Recruitment

The ease or difficulty of recruiting workers was in some instances a reflection of the economic prosperity of the area in which an organisation is based. In general, most organisations reported having a ready supply of applicants for their posts; some who were over-subscribed operate no recruitment procedures beyond a reliance on "word of mouth" referrals. One organiser reported having over 100 applicants on her waiting list for jobs. Some of the organisations in the inner city areas of Dublin commented that the neighbourhoods are so compact that the home helps have very little distance to travel, which is very appealing to workers. Another noted that she has so many applicants that she only hires locally as this saves travel costs. In contrast a non-profit organisation based in a wealthy area with large boundaries described problems with recruiting staff and outlined her extensive efforts to advertise for home helps through supermarkets, local newspapers and church notices. Other recruitment strategies used by organisers included recommendations from PHNs, or employees sent from FÁS, though it was suggested that many from this latter category of workers leave the organisation once they have found a more permanent position. An organiser from a long-settled part of the city suggested that in her area "for many, it's a family tradition" with two or three generations of the same family working in the home help service. Alternate pathways into the job for women from this area, she commented, included "ladies clubs" and other community associations. Many noted that the process of recruitment is often prolonged by the considerable amount of time it can take to get Garda clearance, though one organiser suggested that she only gets it if a worker is going to work with children.

Training

In general the level of training provided to non-profit sector carers is lower than that of the health care assistants and it was clear that no universal standards are adhered to. Some noted that manual handling was mandatory whereas another interviewee whose organisation offers no personal care simply stated that training is not needed for home helps; by way of induction she just accompanies them on their first day. Nonetheless several companies outlined progressive levels of training:

> After interview, each carer gets a starter pack with lots of information on the job. Every few weeks we take a group of new recruits and run a two-hour PowerPoint induction course which makes some safety statements and explains their responsibilities and those of the company. Six months after that they go on a first aid course with the Order of Malta for seven weeks, once a week for three hours. The organisation pays for the course and will cover loss of earnings for any staff who were supposed to be working at the time it is running.

This organisation also ensures its workers are trained in manual handling and will send some of its staff on a palliative care course at a hospice. It postpones any costly training until a carer has gained adequate experience and has shown the necessary commitment to make the investment worthwhile. An organisation operating in the same area runs a half-day training course for new workers, along with basic first aid training in-house if they don't already have it. A sort of peer-mentoring approach is then adopted whereby each new worker is teamed up with and expected to "shadow" an experienced carer for between two and three weeks. The new recruit is initially given relief work until they are eventually allocated their own clients. A number of organisations provide in-depth training only to those who are engaged in personal care. Furthermore, there is a growing movement away from the in-house provision of training, at least beyond the basics, towards the specialised training of small batches of workers through emerging courses in both the public sector, such as Blanchardstown Hospital, and private trainers such as Health Training United Ltd. Other commonly used external trainers include the Red Cross, Order of Malta and the Carers Association.

Monitoring and Complaints

Several of the 19 organisations claimed that although they do not have formal monitoring systems in place, it is fairly standard practice to incorporate this aspect into the schedule of reassessments that most home help organisers or their assistants do every three months. These reassessments evaluate the condition of a client in relation to the level of hours provided. One organiser said that her assistants visit "paying clients" every month. Very few of those interviewed had a formal complaints procedure in place beyond noting that complaints should be directed to them which they will investigate in the first instance. If the client remains unsatisfied, then they may be referred to a director or the committee. Organisers did not believe that the HSE should be involved in this process and an organiser from eastern Dublin made some acerbic comments about a PHN who had taken a client's complaint to the manager of services for older people rather than bringing it directly to her attention.

In general, non-profit managers believed that most complaints revolve around minor innocuous issues such as dissatisfaction with the number of hours allocated, workers turning up late or not working their full hour. Closer inspection of these grievances usually reveals that the worker went shopping for the client, left early to post the clients' mail or the client was mistaken about how much time they were due. Many older people, however, never complain because they are afraid of the ramifications, such as "losing their girl". In cases where a home help is directly criticised by a client, most organisers said they would move the home help to another client, usually without rancour and "start afresh as it doesn't work if two people aren't getting along". It was noted how rare it is to receive a really serious complaint but if they do then the organisation will investigate and talk to all parties involved. For instance, one organisation described receiving complaints about carers "smelling of the drink" and said that if they find that a worker has an alcohol problem they will dismiss them and "blacklist" them with neighbouring home help organisations. A couple of others explained that they occasionally receive accusations of stealing against their workers. One example was given of how a situation escalated into a Garda investigation which was dropped when it was subsequently revealed that the client had dementia. Another said that in 20 years, she had only come across two serious cases of theft. One was proven and action taken, the other went unproven, but she subsequently dismissed the worker anyway on another charge of breaching confidentiality rules (the woman in question had been letting her husband into the house of the client without permission).

The Carers' Stories

In this chapter we have, thus far, focused on the views of the home help organisers in Dublin. This section will explore the work, employment conditions and personal experiences of the workers themselves as described during interviews and focus groups with 20 home care workers employed by non-profit organisations from all over Dublin city. Of the carers interviewed, 11 restricted themselves solely to the roles of home help and companionship, whereas nine had moved into the arena of personal care or a combination of the two roles. Many organisers explained that often workers begin in the job providing domestic care and then gradually and naturally evolve into the personal care role, not least because the client's health deteriorates, but also as they become close acquaintances and friends with their clients. This is by no means a certain trajectory however, with many home helps claiming that they are happy as they are and one even noted that she had originally worked in a private care agency and got tired of the personal care role. She claimed that the hours in the non-profit sector are more relaxed, shorter and better paid than in the private sector.

Terms and Conditions of Employment

Approximately half the workers in the non-profit home care organisations interviewed were unionised. Several said, however, that they were not even aware there was a union that represented home helps. Only one carer talked about regularly attending trade union meetings. She noted that she found them very useful for discussing grievances and problems and that news of developments they hear through these meetings are relayed to the wider carer networks.

The pay rate for all non-profit home care workers has improved dramatically since 2000. Many of these workers started on between £1.00 and £1.50 per hour and are now earning between €12.00 and €14.60 per hour depending on length of service. The majority of interviewees suggested they were now on approximately €13.00 an hour, with time and a half for Saturdays or calls requiring early starts before 7.00 a.m. and late finishes. No difference in payment was identified between those who primarily work in a domestic rather than personal care role, nor did level of training seem a factor systematically reflected in salary. All seemed satisfied that their work was being properly remunerated, though several recalled the difficulties of entering the tax system in 2000 for many workers, including women losing their medical cards, benefits if their husbands were unemployed, and the migration of male carers away from the occupation.

The majority of the 20 home help workers interviewed were working part time. As the following figure demonstrates, six interviewees had approximately full time hours and eight worked between 11 and 20 hours per week.

Figure 5.8: Number of Hours Worked per Week by Home Help Workers

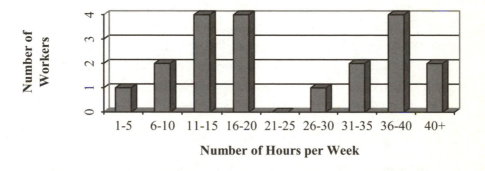

Workers tended to be less clear about the benefits attached to their jobs. Most, but not all, believed that they were entitled to four weeks holiday pay though several said they had "forgotten" to take this or would feel too guilty leaving their clients. Three workers seemed to think that they didn't have a right to holiday pay. Many workers travel on foot to work so travel costs were not always of concern, but several of those who did need to travel said they receive €20.00 a month to cover expenses. Ongoing union-led discussions have also identified a need to implement a wider system of benefits for workers including pension schemes and sick pay. Some organisations do introduce their workers to a private pension scheme, though workers interviewed seemed to that think this would mainly appeal to those at the start of their caring career. Others were un-enthusiastic as they felt that they did not earn enough to pay contributions. Organisers too were sceptical of seeing increases in funding that would allow the roll out of benefits, especially as many of them have been fighting, often unsuccessfully, for their own pensions.

Most problematic according to some organisers was the issue of sick pay and the absences and gaps in service it might cause if implemented. Many workers had no idea about sick pay rights, though one noted that because she is in the tax system she was able to provide a certificate to the social welfare department and receive €148.00 per week whilst she was off work. From the perspective of workers an equal if not more important shortcoming of the current system is that many organisations do not pay them if their client gets sick and is hospitalised or goes into respite care. Some organisers try to compensate for this with additional hours if they have them, but some workers complained that they were simply left without an income, which they believed was unfair if they were available for work. Home helps from one organisation stated that their organiser had recently extended this practice of non-payment further to include situations when they cannot gain access, such as when a client is out of the house, or when (as occasionally happens) a client decides to not allow a carer to enter the property.

Domiciliary Work and Personal Care

Vignette 1: Maureen Donnelly (name changed)

Maureen Donnelly is in her mid-fifties and has worked for the last four years for a non-profit home help organisation in central Dublin. When asked about whether she liked the term "home help" she replied she was very comfortable with it and felt it didn't really matter. If anything, her profession should be called "the listeners" she joked. Maureen had been doing part-time work in another occupation and she felt that the time had come to get another job. Her sister had worked in the home help service some years back and the ties between the local organiser and her family had remained strong so she paid her a visit and a job was arranged. Maureen works five hours a week and starts in the afternoons. "It suits my clients for me to come around this time, especially those who don't get up very early." Her main tasks include cleaning, shopping, doing the laundry, and whatever else she can fit into the hour, though she rarely has to pick up messages as all but one of her clients are mobile. Clients often forget she is only supposed to be there for an hour. One woman she visits lives on the fourth floor of an apartment block and Maureen notes that climbing up four flights of stairs can be time-consuming when returning with the shopping. She visits another client informally on Sundays to drop off a newspaper. She feels that she gets on with her clients but that it can vary from day to day and she is never entirely sure what the situation is going to be when she arrives. Sometimes clients don't want her to leave and she feels dreadfully guilty when she does go. Another client prefers not to see her at all, so goes to the bingo when she is there and leaves the key under the mat. When asked about training, she replied that she doesn't "need it as it's all commonsense", though admits she would consider doing a first aid course if it was free. Maureen likes her job and feels the money is good and the hours flexible. The worst aspects are the clients with alcohol problems or those who treat home helps like cleaners or consider them inferior. Taking a pragmatic approach Maureen summed up her position as a home help, "it's a job like any other — you just have to remember that you are not there to dictate to the clients but that you are a visitor to their house. You mustn't reorganise their furniture or their lives."

This point was mentioned in another focus group where a home help who supports three clients commented on the importance of knowing "where the boundaries lie" and respecting the client's personal space. She went on to say that "sometimes you would love to de-clutter a home, but they like it like that . . . once they have their food and heat, that's my job done." The work tasks home helps were expected to do vary between clients, "mostly talking with one client, another who just wants cleaning,

cleaning, cleaning . . ." Most workers described activities such as picking up prescriptions, pensions, emptying commodes, lighting fires and keeping an eye on health in addition to chores such as cooking, cleaning and shopping. Providing companionship was often thought to be the most important dimension of the job, however.

Of the workers who provide purely domestic duties, none had less than three clients; usually this group of workers had between three and five people on their list. Two of the 11 workers in this category saw more than ten clients each. Taken as an average, each worker within this group would see 5.5 clients.

Figure 5.9: Distribution of Home Helps and Personal Carers by Number of Clients

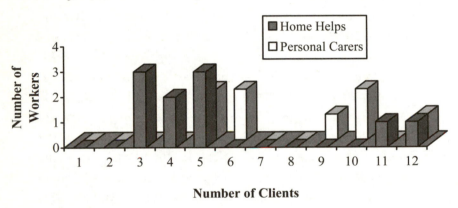

Of the nine workers interviewed from the non-profit organisations who considered their role as primarily providing personal care such as dressing or showering, none saw less than five people and again the most seen was 12.[4] The average number of clients per carer for this category was 7.9, perhaps reflecting greater demand for the "dual" carer role.

---

[4] There were two interviewees, one from each category, who were excluded from these figures. One because she had recently been promoted into a supervisory role and the other because the exact number of clients was unclear from the interview.

Vignette 2: Doris O'Brien (name changed)

Doris has been working in a large non-profit home help organisation in north Dublin for seven years. Most of her workload involves showering her client, helping them to rise and go to bed, and giving respite to family carers. She prefers to be called a "carer" as she feels the term "home help" does not adequately sum up what she does. Now in her forties, her original reason for entering this line of work stemmed from her experience of a death in her immediate family. After the death, Doris decided that caring was her vocation. She said "once you have seen real pain, it helps you to put yourself in the position of others" and noted that she felt this made her a better carer. She usually works over 40 hours a week, though she manages to take off some hours in the afternoons as she spreads this out over seven days. Occasionally she will do evenings and overnight work as her organisation delivers home care packages and she can earn more per hour during these stints. She sees five clients in an average week and has to do a lot of travelling between them as the area she works in is huge. At the moment she visits three clients over the age of 65, a young girl and a young man with a broken neck who requires a substantial number of care hours. Her training included a first aid and a manual handling course. Carers in her organisation are also offered short training courses if they work with certain categories of clients, for instance she used to work with an autistic child and so completed a training session on autism. Her latest client is a young child who recently had a tracheotomy. One night the child began choking and lost consciousness. Doris called 999 and the emergency operator explained how to get the girl breathing again despite the hole in her throat. The child survived and after this incident, she went for a training session with some nurses at a local hospital where they showed her the basics in sorting out the tube. She strongly feels that this sort of training should be offered before a carer takes on a specialist job like this. In general she gets to know her clients well and usually stays with them until they die or go into hospi-

tal. She believes that the best part of the job is making a differ-
ence in people's lives who couldn't manage without her. The
worst aspect is the families who treat her like a servant.

Workers providing personal care discussed the various tasks they carried
out on a daily basis including showering, bathing, dressing, sorting out
medication, companionship, brushing hair and rubbing in ointments. All
said, however, that they operate in a dual role rather than strictly personal care on account of the wasted effort that would be involved in
sending two workers into the same house to do different jobs. The only
male carer interviewed said that men are very much in demand in the
home help service as certain men are more comfortable with another
male helping them with their personal care.

Several dominant reasons for joining the service emerged from the
data. We have already seen from the two vignettes home care workers
who began either through family contacts or in response to a personal
tragedy. The most prevalent pathway amongst interviewees was to have
initially started as an unpaid carer for a neighbour and then be informed
about the possibility of payment by visiting PHNs or other professionals.
Several were recruited directly by home help organisers and others were
attracted by the relatively high levels of pay or the nature and flexibility
of the work. Two came from nursing home or private agency backgrounds. All but three workers had done some basic first aid training,
although some were given more opportunity that others to refresh this
regularly. Twelve out of the 20 home help workers interviewed mentioned receiving manual handling training.

Table 5.1: Previous Care Experience of Workers

Type of Experience	Numbers of Workers
None	10
Unpaid family carers	3
Unpaid neighbourhood carers	4
Nursing home work	1
Private care agency work	1
Foreign nursing experience	1
Total	*20*

The length of experience amongst the non profit organisation workers interviewed varied from one to 27 years. Eight out of 20 had less than five years in the service, but six had over 15 years experience.

Figure 5.10: Length of Service amongst Home Helps Interviewed

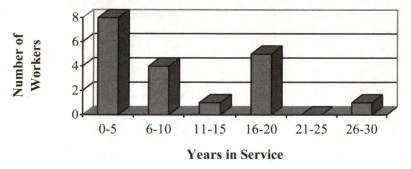

Relationship with Clients

Whilst the majority of carers stressed the positive aspects of the relationships with their clients, such as the friendships that develop and the feeling of self-worth they gain from visiting lonely or vulnerable people who depend upon them, a number of cautionary messages were also conveyed. The first was that some clients are very private and can take a long time to get to know. Families can be difficult, perhaps neglecting their relative, or treating the home care worker badly. One focus group discussed how some clients' family members begin to think the home help is there for the general household rather than the specific client. As one worker put it:

> Sometimes a client will get cranky with the carer, but usually you just have to flow with it and remember they are ill. Sometimes the client will treat the carer as a cleaner, and that's when you give the client the name of a cleaning firm. The same if they ask for something like cleaning the windows. Carers are not covered if they hurt themselves falling off a stool and so if they hurt their back they could end up without a proper income for the time they are off.

In general, the accounts of the relationships between the workers and their clients were very positive and many often referred to the closeness that develops and humour and intimacies shared. One noted that she believed that "in most instances that slice of cake and cup of tea is more important than hoovering the floor". This was especially the case with isolated older clients whose only regular contact with the outside world may be the home help or personal carer. Unfortunately, this relationship in itself can create problems, as some clients start to become over-dependent on their carers, becoming anxious if they are late or calling them at home, or late at night. Workers were divided on whether to give their phone numbers out. One stated that she had learned never to do this from a bad experience when she first started, whilst others felt that they are more comfortable if clients have a means of accessing them, noting they usually give the details of mobile phones, which can be easily switched off. The other major shortcoming of becoming close to the clients is when they get seriously ill or die. Several discussed how difficult this was, "when you go home you continue thinking about them" explaining the sorrow that carers feel at seeing their clients in such poor health, but noting that joking and making them happy can give great satisfaction. One of the worst aspects for some was "when you arrive and the curtains are closed as you worry that something as happened". Many attend the funerals of their clients if they have the opportunity.

Care Workers' Recommendations for Improvements

As each interview or focus group was concluding, the research team asked the participants about how they would like to see things improved for the better. The issue of training was raised several times. It was felt that the training they received was either inadequate or should be refreshed on a regular basis, especially aspects such as first aid training and manual handling "as it's easily forgotten". One worker said she would love to receive more training on a wider range of care issues but noted that asking carers and home helps to go unpaid on lengthy courses was not realistic. Others stated that they are aware of many older people in their communities in Dublin who should receive support, but currently do not get it. It was also mentioned in two focus groups that clients should receive more visits and support from the community nursing service. It was argued that some nurses have bad reputations among the care worker networks. Some nurses were reported as being too forceful with their clients, "they should remember these people are in their eighties", others ignore or unduly delay responding to requests by home helps for their services. One worker said she "asked one nurse to come and cut the nails of a client and it still hasn't happened. Her nails are bending back on themselves". Finally a carer suggested that she was often dismayed at the lack of information older people seem to have regarding their entitlements. She claimed that she is often asked for advice by her clients but that she frequently does not have the information herself.

Conclusions

This chapter has traced the evolution of many of Dublin's non-profit home help organisations from volunteer "good neighbour services" run by religious or community groups to limited companies managed by professional organisers who oversee hundreds of paid staff and clients. It has argued that most have now adopted limited company status and that some, though by no means all, are restructuring their expectations and modes of practice to accommodate landmark changes to the home care industry such as the implementation of home care packages. It has explored the experience of working as a home care organiser, home help or in a dual role that combines domestic and personal care duties, and outlined conditions of employment, recruitment practices, training and the advantages and difficulties of working in this sector.

In 1998 the report *The Future Organisation of the Home Help Service in Ireland* was produced by the Policy Research Centre, National College of Ireland. Its authors, drawing on the views of "managers, providers and beneficiaries", identified a comprehensive list of changes that needed to be made as the service entered the twenty-first century. Their main recommendations were summarised by Haslett, Ruddle and Hennessy (1998) as follows:

1. Clarify the nature of the service provided by home helps

2. Reflect this clarification in training programmes for home helps and home help organisers

3. Further reflect the core nature of the service in the rates of remuneration and conditions of work for home helps

4. Draw up explicit and agreed criteria for assessment of needs of clients which will apply nationally

5. Standardise criteria for entitlement, including carefully considering obligations to all older people in need regardless of their means

6. Determine national guidelines for the level of service provision based on assessed needs

7. Implement an organisational structure for the home help service within the health services

8. Have regard for the inter-dependence of the voluntary organisations and the health boards, with mutual recognition of each other's respective roles and ethos.

How has the situation progressed, eight years after these recommendations were made? The data provided from this section of the study would suggest that whilst progress has been made towards several of these goals, a great deal remains to be done in order to attain them all.

Most obviously achieved is the recognition of the contribution made by workers as reflected in their hourly rate of pay. This has been standardised and improved in recent years and no home care workers made complaints during interviews about financial remuneration. This was not so concerning the wider package of social benefits however, particularly in regard to sick pay and payment whilst a client is in hospital, on holiday, etc. However, the remuneration of the organisers in charge of the service was viewed as not being sufficient. Home help organisers were aggrieved that their benchmarked salaries did not recognise their contributions or workload.

Training was identified as an area requiring substantial improvement. At present, only an informal distinction between the provision of domestic care and personal care exists in many organisations. It is sometimes assumed that workers will organically move from the role of home help to personal carer in the course of their work life, yet many indicated that this was not desirable or that they had made the transition but not received the training necessary to safely and comfortably carry out this role. It is clear that basic courses in health and safety and refresher courses in first aid need to be made available to all home care workers (regardless of their specific role), whilst more specialised training should be given to those working with individuals with more extensive care needs. This should be a standard for any private or non-profit organisation providing home care packages.

Points six, seven and eight continue to be a source of contention for organisers, as they struggle on the one hand to maintain their independent status and negotiate favourable positions in relation to service level agreements and home care packages on the other. The implementation of SLAs is now proceeding apace though many organisers would argue that this is occurring without proper consultation, thus negating point eight. Also not attained is the national level execution of points four and five. What is clear is that the number of hours available to clients varies throughout different parts of Dublin as do practices of collecting contributions. For hours provided under the generic home help budget, assessment and final decisions remain under the control of individual organisers, though this is slowly being challenged by the introduction of a separate stream of funding in the form of home care packages. This point will be explored further in the next chapter that looks at the growth of the private home care industry in Dublin.

Chapter 6

THE MARKET: ROLE IN THE PROVISION OF HOME CARE

Martha Doyle

The private home care industry in Ireland is a grey area in the literature. Since private sector providers have been a part of the Irish care mix for only the last decade or so, there is virtually no information on the size, remit, growth and purpose of this sector. Factors which have contributed to the growth of this sector include changing demographics and economic profiles and the introduction of publicly financed home care packages that are in most cases delivered by private care agencies and companies.

Research Methods

The first step towards understanding the private home care sector involved creating a database of the names of private home care organisations currently operating in the country. In the absence of a centralised information system on the private home care sector, a trawl through the *Golden Pages* and the world-wide web was undertaken. Search terms used included "home care" and "nurses". In many instances an inspection of the advertisement was sufficient to glean whether the company was a nursing agency or a home care provider; however, in uncertain cases the name of the agency was entered into the database. Organisations that only offered nursing services and/or nurses' assistants were disregarded. In total 30 organisations were listed in the database. In order to obtain a preliminary insight into the size and structure of these organisations a short one-page postal survey was dispatched.

A cover letter outlining the aims of the research and the accompanying survey was posted in August 2005. Two weeks after this initial mail-out, a reminder slip was posted to all of the organisations that had not responded. Follow-up phone calls were conducted to ascertain reasons for non-completion (see Table 6.1). Over half of the organisations listed were either non-contactable or did not fit the home care category. Such a finding does not seem to be unusual: a similar exercise carried out in Northern Ireland by the Social Care Council in 2002 (Mathew, 2002) found that over two-thirds of the organisations they had compiled through the *Yellow Pages*, United Kingdom Home Care Association members and interest groups, did not fit into the home care category. It is difficult to surmise why seven of the listed organisations had an out-of-service number. One possible explanation is that these organisations have simply gone out of business (indeed two of the organisations listed in the 2005 *Golden Pages* directory are not listed in 2006). However, in the absence of further research this can only be regarded as a tentative deduction. Moreover, telephone conversations with a number of the providers suggested that the private home care market is in a constant state of flux, with new players entering the market and others leaving or changing their market focus from the supply of home carers to nurses and hospital/nursing-home assistants, and vice versa.

Due to time limitations it was decided at the outset that this study as a whole would focus on the Dublin area. Nonetheless, the private sector postal surveys were dispatched both to Dublin and regional organisations in order to determine the presence of this sector across the country. Two organisations in Dublin declined to complete the questionnaire on the grounds that they were too busy. While exercising a reasonable element of caution it can be assumed that 14 private home care organisations currently operate in Dublin. As Table 6.1 indicates, the number of organisations operating outside the Dublin area is low. However, the numbers below must be regarded as conservative, firstly because the exercise was not an exhaustive search (because all organisations do not necessarily advertise in the *Golden Pages* and the Internet) and secondly, nursing agencies and those delivering nurses' aides were not included. Nonetheless it can be assumed that outside the Dublin area the private sector home care industry does not at the moment have a strong presence.

Table 6.1: Response Rates from Postal Survey

County	Completed	Providers Too Busy to Reply	Telephone No Longer in Service	Retired, No Longer Provides Home Care	Not Applicable, Does Not Deliver Home Care	Total
Dublin	12	2	2	1	3	20
Wicklow	1					1
Cork			2			2
Galway			1			1
Limerick			1			1
Carlow	1					1
Waterford	1				1	2
Kilkenny					1	1
Kildare			1			1
Total	*15*	*2*	*7*	*1*	*5*	*30*

The postal questionnaire dispatched to the private home care directors was a short, one-page survey enquiring about the size and makeup of the organisation. At the end of the survey directors were asked to indicate whether or not they would permit contact from a researcher in the future with a view to providing more detailed information. Beginning in September 2005, directors who had indicated a willingness to engage in further contact and who focused 25 per cent or more of their services on older people were contacted for the purpose of conducting a semi-structured interview. In total nine interviews were conducted. In early February 2006 the director of a private home care franchise that had just entered the market the previous November contacted the research team, and indicated a willingness to be interviewed, bringing the total number of interviews with private home care directors to ten. The interviews with directors expanded upon questions that had been addressed in the survey and sought information about the history and background of the company, employment conditions of staff and issues of concern to the managers of the private home care companies.

Private Home Care — The Directors' Perspective

The following analysis of the private home care sector in Dublin is based on the interviews with both the directors and the care workers. Information gained via the survey (largely depicted in the graphs) was analysed for the ten organisations. The decision was made to exclude the remaining four surveys, since in the absence of semi-structured interviews with the directors of these organisations data could not be equally elaborated, verified or explained. The discussion on the private home care sector first begins with a description of the ten organisations largely gained from the interviews with the directors. The analysis then turns to the work of the carers, largely from their own perspective.

The Two Models of Private Home Care

> I operate on an employer basis so everyone goes through PRSI and PAYE and pays taxes, and gets holiday pay and has all the rights of the employee. — Director, Company Mode

> The client pays the carer then I invoice at the end of every month for the agency fee . . . the girls are self employed basically, I don't have anything to do with their tax or PRSI . . . a lot of them wouldn't be under the bracket of tax cause they wouldn't be doing enough hours. — Director, Agency Mode

While there are fundamental differences between the ten organisations, they all have a similar function: all are delivering home care and have a profit agenda. However, a structural dichotomy (agency versus company) of the private home care system currently operates in Ireland. This is illustrated in Figure 6.1 below.

Figure 6.1: *Agency versus Company Models*

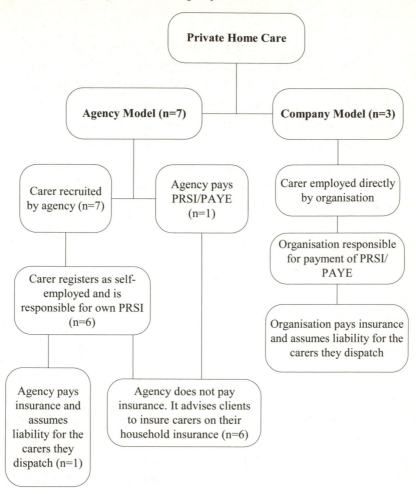

Within the agency model the agency acts as an employment registry, with the view to recruiting and co-ordinating home carers and subsequently matching them with compatible clients. Once this relationship has been established the carer is regarded as self-employed and is recommended to register as such. In the majority of instances responsibility for the insurance of the home care worker is placed with the clients who are advised to extend their household insurance to cover the new worker coming into their home. As well as the initial placement of care worker,

the agency also offers a back-up service which ensures availability of
care for the client; as one director explained succinctly:

> They [the clients] are provided with a solution before they
> know there is a problem, and that's the way it should be, the
> client won't see when Mary [the home care worker] rings in at
> ten o'clock this morning and says she can't make it to Mrs
> Murphy for three o'clock, Mrs Murphy doesn't know this at
> ten o'clock and she's not going to become agitated and say
> who's going to look after me. They're paying us a fee and
> that's our business to get someone in to Mrs Murphy.
> — Director, Agency Mode

The second model in operation is the "company" model: in this model
the private care provider acts as the employer of the carer, employing
and placing the carers, and therefore maintaining responsibility for the
payment of income tax, social security contributions (PRSI) and public
liability insurance. Three of the providers interviewed can be viewed as
operating through the company model, while seven operate through the
agency model.

The distinction, however, between the agency and company model
can get somewhat blurred. For example, one of the agencies interviewed
(while not paying insurance for workers) employs carers directly paying
their PSRI/PAYE and holiday pay, while another who requires carers to
register as self-employed, has an insurance policy which covers all their
carers (see Figure 6.1 above). Noteworthy comments made by Agency
directors included:

> As a company obviously I'm heavily insured but the carers are
> insured under the clients' public liability. — Director, Agency
> Mode

and:

> I would love directives from the government in relation to in-
> surance, but they do need to ask us what is workable. —
> Director, Agency Mode

The failure of a number of agencies to take responsibility for the insurance of the care workers they place is perhaps one of the most contentious issues with respect to the private home care system as it currently operates in Ireland. Only four of the providers interviewed currently insure their care staff for any work-related accidents or damages. One company also has carer's theft cover as well as motor contingency insurance which insures carers to drive a client's car. One director pays public liability insurance of €17,000 a year (for a staff of ca. 50 carers), another incorporates public employee insurance at 4 per cent of the hourly fee, while another pays €50,000 a year for coverage (for a staff of ca. 400 carers). For the remaining six providers, the older client is advised or instructed to take out an insurance policy which insures the carer to work in their home. Generally they are asked to sign a contract which states the agency is not liable for any work-related incidents. Within this study it was not possible to explore whether or not clients do extend their household insurance, however it is highly probable that a considerable number of people do not and hence have no remittance if the carer suffers an injury at work.

Directors operating in the company mode typically have higher overheads and incorporate the cost of administration, supervision, PRSI/PAYE, insurance and holiday pay into the overall fee charged to clients (and/or the HSE where a home care package is in operation). The three directors operating in the company mode voiced frustration at the unequal playing field on which they and the agency providers compete. All three criticised the agency model as it currently operates. Grievances they voiced related to tax, insurance and the clients' inability to obtain tax relief on carers who do not register themselves as self-employed in the agency mode. One director explained:

> The difficulty is that you [the home care recipient] are employing Tom [the agency carer] so if you want to get tax relief you have to register as an employer, the other difficulty is if Tom has an accident in your home, your home insurance may not cover you, cause you are the employer. The other issue is that no tax is being paid by anyone; they call themselves independent contractors, whereas we are paying the tax and they are undercutting us because of this. — Director, Company Mode

These grievances are valid in cases were the care worker has not registered themselves as self-employed (this appears to be the case for the majority of workers in the agency mode) and public liability insurance has not been paid (six of the seven agencies interviewed) and can be viewed as a significant disadvantage of the agency model as it currently operates in Ireland.

Profile of the Private Home Care Organisations

Length of Time in Business

The length of time in the private home care business at the time of the interviews ranged from three months to eighteen years among the ten providers (see Figure 6.2). Three of the businesses had started in the last six months, while six had been in the industry for more than four years. One director claimed to have established the first private home care agency in Ireland in the late 1980s. To this end, it would appear to be correct to characterise the private home care business as a "growth sector".

Figure 6.2: *Length of Time Private Home Care Organisation in Business*

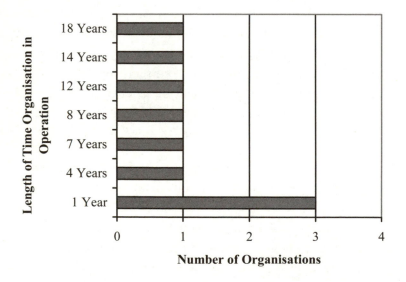

Motivation for Starting Company

The motivation for starting a private home care company varied. For four directors previous experience in the health care area spurred them to set up their own home care company. Personal experience of informal care work and inadequate home care services available to a relative prompted two of the directors to establish their business. Three of the directors were successful business persons in other business sectors and, recognising a profitable niche in the market, decided to branch into the area of home care.

Business Focus

While older persons form the most important single client group for all the providers, the percentage share of older persons (defined here as persons aged 65 or over) in their clientele varies. As Figure 6.3 illustrates, only five of the ten providers focus all of their service specifically on older persons, three focus 75 per cent of their activity on older clients and two focus less than half of their activities on this group. Additional clients of these providers include people with disabilities, convalescent individuals, families and children. Three of the providers interviewed also supply care staff to nursing homes.

Figure 6.3: Percentage of Company Activity Focused on Older Clients

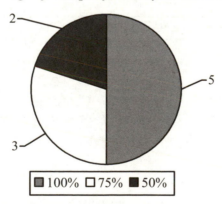

Percentage of Clients Over 65

Size of Workforce and Client Base

The composition of the ten businesses contrasted significantly. As Figure 6.4 below indicates, the number of carers in each business differs substantially: four of the organisations have fewer than 50 care staff, three have between 51 and 100 carers, one 151 to 200 workers, while another has more than 200 carers on their books. The vagueness of these numbers relates to one central characteristic of the home care market; demand for home care services can fluctuate considerably with inevitabilities such as clients going in/out of hospitals, availing of respite beds and passing away, affecting the number of carers required at any point in time. Two of the providers new to the home care market, foreseeing considerable demand for services, expressed confidence that the number of carers in their employment would rise exponentially in the future.

Figure 6.4: Number of Care Staff in Each Organisation

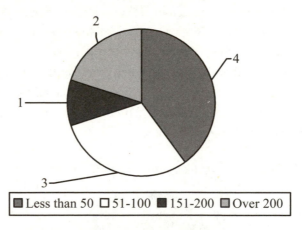

Number of Care Staff per Organisation

The number of clients within each of the organisations also differs considerably: seven cited a client base of fewer than 55 persons, one has ca. 100 clients, another 200, while the largest operator currently has 500 clients (Table 6.2).

Table 6.2: Number of Older Clients per Organisation

Number of older clients	10-15	30	30-40	50	55	150	200	500
Number of organisations	1	2	1	2	1	1	1	1

Nonetheless, all of the interviewees were optimistic about the future growth and expansion of the private home care sector. The overwhelming impression was of a buoyant market where the opportunity to expand is available. Indeed, likely expansion of the service beyond the Dublin area was mentioned by three of the providers. Two of the organisations are newly opened (US) franchises. It is the intention of the directors from these franchises to expand their services beyond the Dublin area; one hopes to open 15 to 20 home care operations throughout the country, the other envisages the opening of six offices. The optimism of one director is reflected in the following statement:

> We would expect to be caring for about 5,000 individuals in about five or six years . . . my expectations have gone higher now than the day we started in terms of how quick we can expand and how much the service is needed. Effectively I would expect to have 20 offices throughout Ireland, if they look after 200 people each that's 4,000 people. — Director, Company Mode

Two directors, however, had reservations about expansion of their business fearing it might jeopardise the overall quality of their service. Another director, commenting on the recent expansion of the private home care sector, was particularly concerned at the entrance of franchised home care operators into the country:

> I don't see them [franchise home care providers] as a threat but I don't think it will do Ireland much good just yet, we need to know what we want, not to be told what we want . . . we could make an expensive mistake . . . give us a little time to develop what is best for us. — Director, Agency Mode

Private Home Care Clients

Clients of the private home care companies can be broadly classified into two groups: fee-paying "independent" clients and "supported" clients in receipt of HSE funding covering all or part of the costs of their care. For this reason there is a diversity of clients within the private home care sector. Two directors expressed surprise at the varied socio-economic profiles of their client bases. Many directors acknowledged that in some cases, delving into the sons' or daughters' income or inheritance is the only way to finance private home care, while one director noted the increasing trend of using the equity of the care recipient's home to fund care. According to one director, some clients have to be gently persuaded by their families to avail of the service or, in some instances, are told that the service is free. Another lamented the fact that some family members take little responsibility for the care of their ageing parent and believed that:

> The families would be giving very little [care], I find if they have a carer in, the odd visit or the odd call, that would be it.
> — Director, Agency Mode

However, this statement can not be taken to reflect the overall level of involvement of families in the care of older relatives as many of those whose older relative is in receipt of formal care continue to provide very high levels of informal care (see Timonen, 2004).

Accessing Clients

> The social workers have to free up the beds . . . so they ring us to see if we can take on the case and they link up with the client to see how the service is going, sometimes they add on more hours, other times they reduce hours. — Director, Company Mode

> I don't advertise, I haven't done for the last year, I didn't need to because of the subvention, the social worker sets it up with ourselves, or passes on the client to us . . . private clients could be one off, or weekends, or waiting for beds in hospitals. — Director, Agency Mode

Accessing clients is not a difficult task for any of the directors interviewed. Clients are usually informed of the provider by a professional source such as a PHN or a hospital social worker, or are referred by a relative or friend directly. All of the directors spoke of the importance of fostering good working relationships with hospital personnel, PHNs, day centres and discharge planners in order to ensure they recommend their organisation to prospective clients. A number of the directors were fortunate to have contacts from their previous work experience in the healthcare field which meant that key personnel within other care settings such as hospitals were aware of their service.

A significant boost to the private home care market in the past few years has been the introduction of publicly-financed home care (home care packages and similar programmes). *For all but two providers HSE home care packages were cited as becoming the main source of their clientele.* The method of payment of the home care packages varies between the different LHO areas across Dublin. For example in the areas covering the former ECAHB the cash entitlement is given directly to some of the individual recipients, who can then select and hire the service they require. In the areas covering the former NAHB, on the other hand, payment is paid retrospectively after service has been accessed and is paid directly to the service provider (Timonen, 2004). Four of the directors interviewed access clients through both systems. The distinguishing feature of these providers is that they all pay insurance which covers the home care worker. The other six providers operating in the agency mode typically only cater for persons who have obtained up-front prospective payments from the HSE. In these instances the older person typically assumes the role and responsibility of employer of the care worker. Unsurprisingly (if insurance and are tax not considered) the agency mode which is significantly cheaper may be more attractive to such clients.

All directors were very welcoming of these new private-public partnerships. The overall impression was that the creation of the home care packages has improved access to services for a group of people who previously could not or did not avail of (private) home care. According to one director the majority of older people are reluctant to pay for private home care, so the provision of home care packages has ensured a considerable number of people in need of care do not go without; this director explained:

> The last thing the elderly want to do is spend their money, I
> know from my own mother, my mother would have died four

years earlier if she had known she was spending as much
money as she was on her home care. . . . If they were paying
for it out of their own money they would be saying no, I don't
need anybody. — Director, Agency Mode

Another cited advantage of the care packages was people's ability to
choose who they would like to receive care from (although admittedly
the degree of freedom of choice varies between the prospective/client-
centred and retrospective/provider-centred models, with the former in
principle allowing greater choice). According to one director this intro-
duces an element of healthy competition among the private companies
and, in some areas, between the private and non-profit home care providers. However, the extent of true competition naturally depends on the
availability of willing providers in the area. In rural areas outside Dublin
it can be difficult to find any, or more than one, provider. A common
sentiment expressed among the interviewees was the need for people to
be better informed of their entitlements to these packages.

Grievances voiced in relation to the care packages included difficulty
with the processing of HSE payments and the splitting of home care
grants between the non-profit and private providers which, according to
two directors, disrupted continuity of care. Allocation of the packages
was queried by another director. On numerous occasions, this director
has questioned the specific allocation of hours to certain clients who did
not seem to warrant the care or else had adequate finances to pay for private care. To avoid such inequities this director advocated a means-
tested system.

Publicly financed home care is the mainstay of business for a number
of private home care providers. Indeed for three of the providers it would
seem that accessing wholly private clients is a relatively small adjunct to
their core service, which is the provision of state-funded home care. One
provider, who is very optimistic regarding the future development of
publicly financed private home care, was of the belief that ultimately the
private companies will be the predominant providers with non-profit organisations playing an ad-hoc support role:

Looking at the [United] States, I think there is only two ways;
the HSE decides to professionally run a service and they pro-

vide the home care people to do that themselves, from listen-
ing to them that is not where they want to go, they want to
have service level agreements with organisations like ourselves, and say you have to do this in terms of training and supervision, once you do all of those things, I'll get you to do it
at that price. And I think that's the way it's going to go . . . and
I would see the voluntary organisations just visiting people
when they can, rather than being part of an organised care
plan. — Director, Company Mode

Assessment of Clients

Assessment of HSE clients is generally conducted by HSE employees
such as the PHN or social workers. They recommend the amount of cash
or services which they deem the person should be entitled to.

Assessment of the care needs of fee-paying (fully private) clients
seems to be carried out in a rather rudimentary fashion. One company, an
exception to the norm, has employed an intake assessor and a client care
coordinator who assess the clients' needs in their home environment.
While some of the other providers do make an initial home visit to discuss the service, none use any structured assessment tool to ascertain
care needs. One director commented that often a family reacting to a recent setback will over-estimate the amount of care a person requires. In
such instances the director tries to persuade the family otherwise, however this director voiced a concern that there is a dangerous trend in the
private home care industry to give into this, or to "hard sell" the need for
maximum care.

Correct matching of clients with carers was argued to be a high priority by all of the private home care providers, although this was often arrived at on the basis of a telephone call or left to the discretion of the
carer who paid the first visit to the client's home. Matching may not always be correct first time round, clashes of personality and tempera-
ments are inevitable in some situations; as one director pointed out:

You're not going to always get it right first time round, matching up the carers and clients . . . sometimes the clients do come
back after a length of time . . . on occasion clients will say you

know that girl that came on relief, can we get her again? —
Supervisor, Agency Mode

One provider uses a five-page application form which contains information on the carer's hobbies, interests and the type of service they would
like to give. This information is then cross-referenced on the computer
with potential clients to achieve a good match. However, such close attention to matching clients and carers is somewhat exceptional.

Quality Standards

Training Private Home Carers

In a market where high-dependency clients are now remaining in, or returning to, the community, the training of staff and subsequent monitoring of work practises are extremely important.

Overwhelmingly directors stated that all carers, prior to commencement of work, will have some degree of knowledge of manual handling,
first aid or work in a nursing home. The content and extent of this train-
ing/experience however differs considerably and in some cases may be
quite dubious. One director stated that a minimum of two years work
experience is required of all carers, however a subsequent interview with
one of their employees, whose qualification consisted of a five-day training course, indicated that this requirement is not necessarily strictly adhered to at all times. Divergent attitudes towards training are elucidated
in the comments below:

> Because a lot of it is not strenuous, a lot of it is just assisting
> someone having a bath or just being there in case they fall, the
> need for training isn't that great. . . . I have cases where they
> would get progressively worse and would get a new bed and
> hoist, whoever is providing the hoist gives them training and
> shows them how to use it, which would be the PHN, they would
> show them how to work them. — Director, Agency Mode

> If you take companionship, they would have CPR training,
> manual handling training even though we don't get involved in
> manual handling issues just to be aware of the training issues,

> safety, dignity of the person, then graduating up to personal
> care. — Director, Company Mode

The amount of training that organisations are prepared to invest in their staff varies significantly, and in some cases the attitude can be characterised as bordering on lackadaisical. Aside from the above quoted organisation that intends to offer FETAC training to its care staff, two other providers have introduced *voluntary* training in subjects such as manual handling and caring for people with Alzheimer's disease.

It has been argued that often the quality of care work from the perspective of the care recipient is more a consequence of the interpersonal skills of the carer rather than their professional skills set *per se*, nonetheless minimum training standards to safeguard both the client and the worker must be enforced. One director working in the home care industry for more than a decade, while advocating increased training for home care workers, cautioned that such a "professionalisation" of the workforce must be done in a slow and conscientious manner:

> We have to give them confidence, these are women that may
> not be very positive about themselves, they have to be encour-
> aged to develop themselves, if you come in with too high of an
> academic training it worries them a lot so you have to start off
> gradually to encourage them, and then they go forwards from
> there. — Director, Agency Mode

All of the directors were reluctant to finance the costs of carer training. Updating of skills was seen by three of the agency directors to be the sole responsibility of the individual. Among these directors a carer's desire to update or refresh skills was viewed as an individual choice which they could self-finance and pursue independently. With the majority of home carers working on a part-time basis, often working in other jobs, the allegiance of a carer to an organisation was argued as being somewhat ambiguous.[1] This sometimes ambivalent relationship coupled with

---

[1] In contrast to this director's belief, it must be noted that of the 23 home carers interviewed in the research almost three-quarters had worked for the organisation for between 1 and 10 years.

the fluctuating demands of the home care industry was cited as a disincentive to "provider-financed" training. While three directors were very much in favour of minimum training standards, they also intimated that they would require state subsidies to fund this training. One of the directors also working in the nursing home industry noted that the government subsidises training for nursing home staff, and expressed the hope that the government would pay similar subsidies for the training of home care workers.

Monitoring of Home Carers

> We monitor them on the roster and then we do spot-checks . . .
> At the end of the sheet [client feedback form] it says are you
> satisfied with the quality of service provided, there's also a
> complaint form so if they have any problems they just fill in
> the appropriate sheet, and if they don't sign the appropriate
> sheets we don't get paid by the HSE as we give in these sheets
> when we claim the hours. — Director, Company Mode

Subsequent monitoring and supervision of carers once they have begun work varies considerably. Five of the providers could be regarded as focusing closely on service delivery and monitoring. One director makes personal visits to each of her clients every four to six weeks. Similarly another dedicates a week each month to seeing their clients. Another has employed a nurse who acts in a supervisory capacity, while another has employed two people to ensure customer satisfaction and quality monitoring. One of the newly established organisations, eager to concentrate on supervision and monitoring, explained that they have installed a computerised system for monitoring carers, the first of its kind in Ireland. When a carer arrives or leaves the client's house, they clock in by use of the client's phone, which recognises the number and logs the times. For the other five agencies the monitoring of workers is not routine. In some instances phone contact is the only form of communication between the home care organisation and the client.

Regulation

In light of the financial rewards which can be gained with the increase in publicly financed home care, it is not surprising that all of the directors who intend to focus almost exclusively on HSE clients called for increased regulation of the private home care sector. A concern about the unregulated structure of the sector was voiced by five directors. With an increase in publicly financed home care contracts it was deemed that adequate quality monitoring will be critical. Improved transparency, accountability and regulation were called for:

> I'd like to see an association here in Ireland where we can have a set of rules and regulations about what's expected, we would like to work with the HSE, we have already done that in this area to get service level agreements with the HSE. . . . I don't mind competitors but I want competitors on the same level. . . . I'd hate if our name were associated with an industry that's delivering a shoddy service. — Director, Company Mode

Another noted that:

> There are a lot of agencies out there that I would call matching agencies . . . we are trying to get the government to regulate what's going on, cause in that scenario there's no training, there's no supervision, there's no background checks . . . we think there's a Leas Cross scenario out there in home care. — Director, Company Mode

As the statements above illustrate, directors in the company mode advocated fundamental changes in the regulation and monitoring of home care agencies, stating that they had grievances with the self-employed nature of care staff within the agency model, meaning agencies could undercut prices and responsibility for insurance is transferred to the client.

One provider emphasised that it is important that private home care providers get the standards correct and "are not in it for the quick buck". For this provider regulation in the form of training was viewed as the preferable option. This director has taken active steps to try to establish a federation of private and non-profit care organisations, however they are still in the embryonic phase of the process:

> While we are commercial you always have to have that
> thought that it is a social element in society . . . so I am quite
> concerned now Ireland is a much wealthier country, funding is
> given for various things and it does seem that a lot of the fund-
> ing will be partly subcontracted to private industries, and I
> think it is really important that now as it is still a quite embry-
> onic business that we get the standards correct now. — Direc-
> tor, Agency Mode

Another director was sceptical of the HSE's willingness to regulate the home care sector. This director believed that a disincentive from the HSE perspective would be the fact that similar regulations would have to be enforced in the non-profit sector which would have considerable cost ramifications:

> I think when they get around to looking at it, they will realise
> you can't have standards in just the private sector, you will
> have to have them in the public sector. Just take training alone,
> if the HSE has to turn around and train all their home helps to
> a basic standard that's going to cost them a fortune. — Direc-
> tor, Company Mode

It is important to acknowledge that increased regulation, with the intention of improving standards, will lead to increased costs associated with train-ing and monitoring, which subsequently can translate into higher service fees. Such increases in the cost for private home care may force some fee-paying (i.e. fully or partly private) customers to consider other home care alternatives within the grey market where no over-sight or protection is guaranteed. In some countries, this "flight to the black market" has been successfully combated with the help of tax regimes that incentivise all home care users to seek tax relief. Such tax incentives can help to counter-act the emergence of an unregulated black market in home care if they are available only for those who use registered providers.

Financing

Cost of Private Home Care

All of the ten providers offer 24-hour care seven days a week. However, for most companies 24-hour live-in care is only one kind of service offered and tends to be fairly marginal in comparison with daytime and evening work that is usually delivered in minimum blocks of two or more hours.

Due to the dichotomy of the agency and company models, and other factors such as the rates of pay for workers and the desired profit margin, the cost of private care for older people can vary markedly. Many of the private care agencies spoke of the need to offer a low-cost high-quality service, even if it comes at the expense of lower rates of pay for their care staff. Table 6.3 outlines the prices charged by the ten organisations — prices quoted are weekday prices only. The stipulation of a minimum number of hours means that in some instances costs are not strictly comparable. Noteworthy is the fact that one company that employs carers directly (paying PRSI/PAYE, holiday leave and insurance) is able to offer care at a competitive rate of €19.00 for one hour or €32.00 for two hours — only €3.00 more than three other agencies that do not factor PRSI, PAYE, holiday pay or insurance into their rates. This calls into question the argument (voiced by some of the agencies) that directly employing the care workers leads to escalating costs and uncompetitive rates.

Within the agency model, the method of invoicing clients differs. In some instances the client pays the worker cash in hand weekly and the agency fee on a monthly basis, while other agencies invoice the client on a monthly basis. Loyalty to the agency is important in the former arrangement, with one director who remunerates in this way stating that half of all clients will suggest to workers that they negotiate their own private contract to avoid paying the agency fee. By and large, however, the carers do not acquiesce.

Table 6.3: Cost of Private Home Care

Cost of Service – Monday to Friday Only
Company Mode
€18.50 per hour depending on level of care up to €22.00 per hour (minimum 3 hours)*
€18.75 per hour depending on level of care up to €22.95 per hour (minimum 3 hours)*
€16 per hour (minimum 2 hours) €19 per hour (1 hour)*
Agency Mode
€22.26 for 1 hour plus 21 % VAT, €29.11 plus 21% VAT for 2 hours care
€23.60 for 2 hours (minimum 2 hours)
€28.40 for 2 hours (minimum 2 hours)
€20 plus agency fee, plus VAT for 2 hours (minimum 2 hours)
€22.36 for 1 hour; €29.11 for 2 hours
€21.32 per hour (minimum 4 hours)*[2]
€30.75 for 2 hours (minimum 2 hours) plus once-off admin fee of €65

A recent challenge which many of the providers have to contend with is the expansion of the grey home care market. Increased competition with the grey market has resulted from an influx of non-Irish workers providing home care at lower rates. In the course of a telephone conversation, the director of a Dublin home nursing agency stated her belief that many people are seeking alternatives to the lack of Health Board provision of home help by getting au-pair, housekeeping or nanny agencies to look after elderly parents. She believes that some non-Irish nurses employed in medical care work during the day also work at night, sleeping over in an older person's home, bathing them and ensuring that they have adequate food. This sentiment was also echoed by one of the directors interviewed:

> A lot of people are saying to me when the patients are leaving hospitals, there are so many non-nationals in the hospitals, that they are saying, "if you want anyone at home to work at night

---

[2] Includes insurance.

or anything like that, here's my number", and they always have an aunt or uncle or brother or sister available. . . . But they are undercutting everyone. — Director, Agency Mode

A similar sentiment was expressed by another director in relation to live-in care:

I do find the twenty-four hour live-in care is going down, I think it's to do with the non-nationals, they are going in for half the price. . . . I know from clients, people who would come to me looking and then would come back to me and say I got a Filipino for half the price. — Director, Agency Mode

Of the interviews carried out among the private home care workers, two of the non-Irish carers and one of the Irish carers had previously undertaken this kind of care work in the grey market. Three of the providers stated that increasingly they are finding themselves in direct competition with non-Irish carers who are able to drastically undercut the cost of live-in care. Live-in work is currently the preserve of the private sector in Ireland: neither home care assistants nor non-profit sector home helps offer this kind of service. One agency has anecdotal evidence of non-Irish workers offering live-in services for as little as €450 per week. However, providers have been quick to respond to this by reducing the number of carers serving an individual client, with the workers getting paid a weekly rate rather than an hourly rate. One provider spoke of reducing live-in care costs from €2,000 to €1,000 a week, another from €1,400 to €1,030.[3] Rates of €650, €1,000, €1,030, €1,300, €1,400, €1,600 were quoted by five agencies.

VAT Payments

We don't employ care staff, the client pays the care staff and partly the reason for that is the VAT situation, if you're a charitable organisation you don't charge VAT but a commercial organisation has to charge at twenty-one per cent . . . there are some companies taking the chance and not paying it. — Director, Agency Mode

---

[3] Excluding Saturday and Sunday.

I would like to see the Department of Health, Revenue and Social Welfare getting together and working out a practical solution to the VAT. — Director, Agency Mode

The problem is that the legislation doesn't say whether VAT is on the whole service or just the agency fee. — Director, Company Mode

We don't pay VAT because we are a charitable organisation. — Director, Company Mode

Inconsistencies abound in relation to the payment of VAT with the issue appearing unresolved in policy terms. Many directors feel ill-informed about their legal obligations. Two agencies spoke of hiring consultants to clarify their tax requirements. However, in each case, they were unable to adequately clarify their responsibility. Many were unclear whether they have to pay VAT on just the agency fee or the entire service. One director stated that they charge VAT on the agency fee but not on payroll costs, because the business is in "the medical field" and therefore VAT exempt. Another stated that they pay no VAT because their company is a charitable company. Another director has been informed that the care service industry is exempt from paying VAT. One director charges VAT on the overall cost of care.

One director called for the employed/self-employed relationship to be clarified as soon as possible stating that if this was sorted their agency would employ people directly. Calls for an affiliation of agencies to be brought in by the HSE with a single set of rules and regulations in relation to the issues of pay, insurance and PRSI were voiced by a number of the directors. An irritant for one director was the fact that nurses are non-VAT-able but home carers are not. Another director questioned why people paying for home care were only entitled to tax relief to a maximum of €30,000,[4] since this cut-off point does not apply when paying for nursing home care.

---

[4] This was increased to €50,000 in 2006.

Obligation to Purchase Blocks of Care

All of the organisations stipulate minimum blocks of care. Only two providers offer care in a minimum of one hour blocks, three deliver care in a minimum of two-hour blocks, another in three-hour blocks and another in four-hour blocks. The two or three hour requirement reflects the fact that working in shorter blocks is not deemed feasible or profitable for the care workers who would end up spending too much time in transit between the clients.

While acknowledging the economic practicality of stipulating care in a minimum of two-hour blocks, from the perspective of the client this requirement is often far from ideal, especially when the agency/company and care worker have rigid definitions of the kind of work (personal care only) that they are prepared to do. Given that in many instances people are firstly, reluctant to pay for care and secondly, may not require additional companionship, the enforcing of minimum time periods is a notable disincentive in employing private home care. Four of the directors spoke of having to refuse prospective clients service because their care needs did not necessitate two or three hours of care. The statement below illustrates the impracticality of this stipulation from the perspective of the client:

> I had a lady on yesterday morning and she's been looking after her husband for the last twenty-five years who had a stroke and she just got to a point where she would like someone to go in and just help get him up, she can't physically pull him up, and she said but that would only take twenty minutes, and we have a minimum of two hours, so the woman said could she [the carer] wash out the bath, and bathroom floor, and hoover . . . you know! And she said well I need to get value for me money; well, I said, you'll have to go somewhere else. — Director, Agency Mode

Vying for HSE clientele means that each provider has to make itself as attractive as possible. A number communicated the need to streamline services and offer higher degrees of flexibility, relinquishing their stipulation of service delivery in the minimum of two- or three-hour blocks to HSE clients. One provider has been accommodating in this respect and has taken on HSE packages in slots of 20 to 30 minutes at a significantly reduced cost. Unfortunately, however, this is not available to private fee-paying clients. Another organisation that has a stipulation of a minimum of three hours a day has agreed that time can be split into two 1.5 hour shifts for HSE clients.

Liaison with Non-profit and Public Sector Providers

Liaison between the "non-profit" and "for-profit" home care sectors appears to be virtually non-existent. Overall it would seem that the private sector employers are ill-informed about the work of their non-profit counterparts. Some hinted that they see themselves in direct competition with one director complaining that they compete on unequal terms as the non-profit organisations do not have to pay 21 per cent VAT:

> How can charitable and commercial organisations work hand in hand when there are a different set of rules? — Director, Agency Mode

Another director believes they are in direct competition with the non-profit home care organisations when trying to recruit well-trained Irish workers and commented that:

> The challenge is to get trained staff, competing with the HSE on a salary differential, getting Irish carers, as a lot of older people prefer people of their own nationality, getting carers and trained carers will become more difficult as the sector expands. It all ties back into salary supports, if there was more government support, we could pay at the HSE home help rate, then we are obviously going to get a better calibre of person. — Director, Company Mode

Another director was under the mistaken impression that the non-profit organisations are run on a purely voluntary basis, i.e. that staff are not paid. Two providers were of the impression that the non-profit organisations are not in a position to cope with the current demand for home care from the HSE. Both of these directors believed that ultimately the service level agreements will flourish and the private sector will emerge as the predominant provider:

> I have been told by a few people in the HSE that it [the non-profit sector] is under a huge amount of pressure and that it's not able to cope . . . I've talked to three people in the HSE that can see it coming to an end. . . . A few have said once [current organiser] retires that voluntary agency is just going to fall apart. — Director, Company Mode

Noteworthy were the comments of one director, which highlighted the stretched resources and finances the non-profits organisations have to operate within. Ironically the contracts which this provider intends to negotiate with the HSE will stipulate minimum time periods, a luxury which is inconceivable for the non-profit organisations:

> We would aim that the average client would access eighteen/ twenty hours a week, we have a minimum of three hours a day. I notice from talking to home helps, their average home help hours would be ten hours a week, my own mother-in-law, she gets thirty minutes a day five days a week, which is inadequate. The problem with the HSE home help system is that it's a numbers game, they have big volumes of people who need care . . . it's all budget driven, and it's not driven by the needs of the person in the home. — Director, Company Mode

Another director wondered if the non-profit sector as it currently functions is too "top heavy". This director believed that a reshuffling of the non-profit managers may be a cost-effective exercise, and questioned:

> Are we getting an overlap, when we are paying CEOs [meaning: organisers] in every one of these organisations [non-profit home help organisations], when there are twenty CEOs would ten be sufficient — are they top heavy? — Director, Agency Mode

Profile of the Workforce

The population of private home care workers is a heterogeneous one, with a diversity of ages, ethnic backgrounds and skills. Carers are predominantly female; only one company employs males, as they are "particularly suited for physically demanding work" and as some (male) clients prefer a male carer. While many clients seem to have a preference for carers who are somewhat older, generally the age range of the carers is between 30 and 65. The ethnicity of the workforce varies considerably across the various providers (Figure 6.5). In one organisation 95 per cent of staff is non-Irish, two have between 51 to 75 per cent non-Irish carers, and another two have between 26 and 50 per cent, while five of the organisations have less than 25 per cent non-Irish staff, one of whom stated categorically that they only employ Irish workers. Organisations that employ large numbers of non-Irish workers tend to draw on workers from a fairly small number of countries. Countries most frequently mentioned were Poland, South Africa, Nigeria and the Philippines (Table 6.4).

Figure 6.5: Proportion of Non-Irish Carers

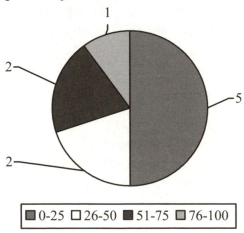

Percentage of Non-National Carers

Overall, recruitment difficulties were not cited with some directors receiving 50 to 60 applications weekly. There was an almost unanimous agreement that previous skills or experience in the area of care for older persons was imperative for someone's job application to be considered. One provider, however, stated that they will consider those with no prior experience in the area provided that the applicant is prepared to work as an unpaid volunteer in a nursing home for three to four days per week for three weeks. Minimal advertising seems to be required, with advertisements in the *Golden Pages* and word of mouth sufficing in most instances. Finding staff to work evenings, nights or weekends does not seem to pose any difficulties. Two of the directors said that a large proportion of their staff are lone parents with young children, for whom night-time work can be preferable.

Table 6.4: Main Country of Origin of non-Irish Carers by Organisation

Organisation	Main Country of Origin of Non-Irish Workers by Organisation
1	South Africa, England, Scotland, Poland and Philippines
2	Not applicable – has no non-national workers
3	Zimbabwe, Nigeria, South Africa, Eastern Europe
4	South Africa, Nigeria, Zimbabwe, Philippines, Sweden, Britain
5	Eastern Europe
6	Poland
7	Philippines
8	Philippines
9	Philippines, South Africa, Nigeria, Europe
10	Poland

> The criteria I use with the girls is would I let that person look after my mother and if I have any doubt whatsoever I just won't take them on. I have to be very careful Irish or not . . . it's still a bit nerve-wrecking with references and that you can only go on what the referees are telling you, I won't accept a written reference or anything like that. — Director, Agency Mode

The inability to adequately vet prospective workers was mentioned by a number of the directors as an issue of concern. On 23 September 2004,

Brian Lenihan, TD, Minister of State with Special Responsibility for Children, announced the provision of additional staff resources for the Garda Central Vetting Unit to enable the Garda Síochána's vetting services to be extended to all persons working with children and vulnerable adults. This meant that theoretically home care providers would be able to vet prospective staff. However, with a workforce of just 30 Gardaí, the demand for Garda checks from employers working with children as well as adults is high, and as a result the wait for checks may be quite lengthy. Two directors have employed private investigators to overcome the difficulty of such lengthy waits, one of whom goes as far as doing credit checks.

A number of directors intimated that some clients indicate a preference for an Irish carer. Three directors acknowledged the difficulty of attracting Irish workers. According to one director, "the Irish psyche is not in tune with home care" because it is considered a demeaning job by many. This director went on to state that there is a problem with getting recognition for the value and status of home care work which is not viewed as a profession. According to one director the welfare system does not lend itself to Irish workers entering the care field:

> They would say I can't work cause I have this allowance and
> if I do this it will damage that . . . so the social welfare system
> needs to be addressed in the context of caring for the elderly,
> cause there are people out there who could give time, but are
> stopped because of other fears. — Director, Agency Mode

Non-Irish care staff on the other hand are in abundance. One director reported receiving 12 to 20 calls weekly from non-Irish people looking for employment, while another receives 8 to 10 such calls daily. It was noted that in many instances these non-Irish workers are highly skilled and have worked in nursing homes or the care industry previously. Acknowledging the skills of many Filipino workers, one director called for a change in the work permit regulations to enable care agencies to get work permits for non-Irish staff. Similarly, another director new to the market would consider bringing trained workers from Poland if they have recruitment difficulties. In light of the changing composition of the Irish care workforce, one director foresees a situation whereby Irish care workers will find themselves in direct competition with highly skilled non-Irish workers:

> Non-national people are very well trained, they are in a new country, they want to make a living and they make the best of opportunities . . . if the Irish economy changes there are [non-national] people who are . . . far better trained and far more willing to work and they are going to be the people who will get the work. — Director, Agency Mode

However, a minority of the providers were hesitant about employing non-Irish workers, due to perceived cultural differences, previous negative experiences, language difficulties and in some instances a reluctance by the client to have a non-Irish carer. In relation to the latter, however, the perception prevailed that in recent years clients have interacted with an increasing number of non-Irish workers in hospitals and other spheres of life and are gradually getting accustomed to this new population of workers.

Private Home Care Work — The Carers' Perspective

We now turn to examining private home care work from the perspectives of the carers themselves. This discussion draws for the most part on the interviews with the carers.

Methods

Private home care directors interviewed were asked at the conclusion of the interview whether they would be willing to help in arranging interviews with their carers for the purposes of the research. In the majority of cases they indicated a willingness to arrange such a meeting. Unfortunately, however, interviews with carers were not as easy to arrange as anticipated. Afternoon focus group meetings were scheduled, but numbers in attendance were low. Reasons given for the lack of responsiveness to interview invitations were "too busy", previous participation in research projects or a lack of interest. Nonetheless, after continued efforts a total of 23 private home care workers were interviewed from six of the ten organisations. Six of these were one-on-one interviews, while the remainder took the form of small focus groups (groups of two, four and five).

Home Carers' Characteristics and Background

Duration of Employment with Current Company

Of the twenty-three private sector home carers interviewed, 15 were Irish and eight non-Irish.

The length of time carers worked with their current organisation varied from two weeks to 13 years, 14 carers worked for the agency a year or less, seven worked between three and seven years, and two for more than 10 years. (see Figure 6.6)

Figure 6.6: Number of Years Carer Worked for Home Care Organisation

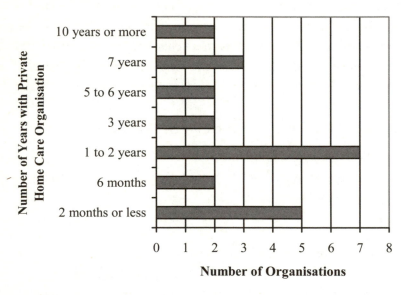

Previous experience and training varied considerably among the 23 carers interviewed (see Table 6.5). Twelve carers had previous experience of working in either a nursing home or hospital, two of whom are qualified nurses. Two carers had previously worked as health care assistants in the former health boards and a further two carers had worked as home help/private carers. Two carers who had no previous experience in the home care area prior to commencement of the job completed training courses while in the job. Only one carer had no training, however this carer only delivered companionship care at weekends.

Table 6.5: Previous Training and Qualifications of Private Home Care Workers

Type of Experience	Number of Workers
Work experience includes work in a hospital or nursing home	12
Worked as HCA	2
Worked as home help or private carer	2
Training receieved during job	2
Self-financed training which was completed before job	4
No training	1
Total	*23*

Four of the non-Irish carers had completed self-financed courses prior to commencement of their jobs. Such courses are available in numerous schools throughout Dublin. These courses range in length from one day to six months and can cost from €80 to €600. One carer who had completed a three week course costing €450 for three weeks (plus €40 for the purchase of a nursing uniform which is mandatory), commented that ten of the 12 students on her course were non-Irish. The nationalities she identified included South African, Nigerian and Indian. One director interviewed also mentioned the increased supply of people who have completed such courses, and was anxious about their accreditation. Since many of these schools have a for-profit agenda, this director believed that an accreditation board should be established which would ensure minimum training standards.

Reasons for Entering the Job

> The majority of carers are not in the job for the money, cause in fairness it's not the best paid job in the world, a lot are there cause they really enjoy what they do and they know they are doing a really good job and the people are happy with them.
> — Home Care Worker, Company Mode

The reasons for entering private home care work were largely practical, altruistic or financial. Practical reasons included the flexible nature of the work, which suited those with children, those undertaking study and, for four carers, it reduced the pressure and stress often associated with other work.

An altruistic caring disposition and the desire to assist the needy was a central motivation for ten of the care workers. A desire to help and care for the old was voiced by these carers who explained that they felt protective of their clients and found care work fulfilling and rewarding. Six of the carers had delivered care informally to acquaintances, grandparents, children and parents and realised they had an affinity with the role of carer, three compared it to the work of a mother caring for her children. Two of these workers later went on to work in hospitals, while a further two worked as health care assistants in the community. Due to a health condition one of the carers working as a health care assistant had to quit work and entered the private sector as work there was more flexible and somewhat lighter and less personal care oriented. One interviewee who had combined work as a health care assistant with private care work for a period, discovered a preference for the wider spectrum of clients in the latter, and began working full-time for the private sector.

Twelve of the carers had worked in a hospital/nursing home before beginning work as a private home carer. A comparison between these two environments was made by seven of the workers. In the main, nursing home work was seen as more restrictive and less desirable than work in the community. Nursing home work was regarded as more stressful, more exhausting and psychologically demanding, often working with limited resources and staff shortages. Two of the carers were qualified nurses. For one of them work as a nurse was too pressured and she believed one-on-one work in people's homes was more rewarding. Another carer, who qualified as a nurse in South Africa, explained that it would cost €15,000 to transfer her degree qualification. One carer, however, who is also registered with a nursing agency, found nursing home work more attractive than home care work. She believed that there was more back-up support in a nursing home, and the issues of security and vulnerability to violence and work-related injury were of lesser concern to workers in institutional care settings.

"Financial reasons" was the stated motive for one non-Irish interviewee becoming a carer. She had previously worked in a number of jobs in Dublin before working as a carer, including work in a warehouse, packing and as a cleaner. She was having difficulty finding employment and therefore decided to invest in a three week course in home care. Following training her preferred choice would have been work in a nursing home, but she believed these jobs were harder to access without experience. It was her belief that home care work pays relatively well in comparison with other semi-skilled jobs and thus for the moment she views her work as a live-in carer as a comparatively lucrative entry-level role, which she hopes to be promoted from. Another woman was faced with the prospect of a reduced income when left widowed. In her experience working long hours including night-time shifts could yield a relatively comfortable income.

Three of the carers explained that they will not continue in this line of work indefinitely and were undertaking courses of study. However, one of these carers would like to combine care work with office work once she is qualified.

Private Home Carers' Work

> The first thing is that you could work with the elderly twenty-four seven, there are so many people needing support, my working day would start at ten in the morning and could go on to ten in the night. — Home Care Worker, Agency Mode

The job of a home carer is a versatile one. Services available from the private home care sector include domestic care, personal care, day sitting/companionship service, night sitting service, night waking service, respite care and live-in care. Tasks are broad-ranging with private home carers generally working in a dual capacity, delivering light domestic care and personal care (see Figure 6.7 below for summary of different tasks).

Figure 6.7: Private Home Care Services on Offer

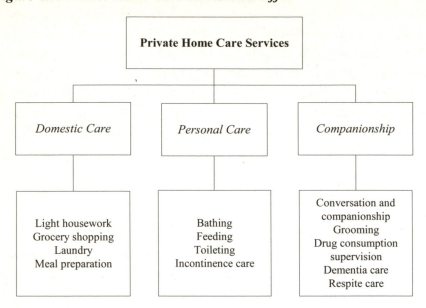

Medical conditions of the clients relayed by the carers included strokes, Multiple Sclerosis, paralysis, Dementia, respiratory problems, psychiatric illness, mobility difficulties and anxiety problems. While some workers focused more on personal care than domestic work, tasks generally included food preparation, light housework, accompaniment to medical appointments, supervision and companionship. Personal care generally related to helping persons out of bed, help with dressing, prompting medication, bathing, application of ointments, showering and grooming.

Paramedical care such as dispensing medication, wound dressing and administering injections is not permitted by the majority of the organisations. However, two organisations state in their information pamphlets that wound dressing is available. Only two interviewees said that they administer medication, one of whom, a qualified nurse (but employed as a carer), administers injections.

All the private home care organisations offer light housework. Domestic care, while broadly fitting within the remit of a carer's work, was viewed by the majority of the carers as secondary to the role of home carer. Five carers mentioned that it is important to draw the line in relation to the amount of house cleaning which can be provided. However three did suggest that in certain cases they will be lenient and do additional cleaning:

> You are not going to clean the windows, but if somebody is bed-bound and looking at a dirty window you would clean it.
> — Home Care Worker, Agency Mode

> I don't think there are many carers who won't hoover for their client, but it's a fine line. — Home Care Worker, Agency Mode

The majority of the private home care companies and agencies list laundry as a service they provide on their information pamphlets; however only two of the carers mentioned laundry among their key tasks. One of the carers said she would refuse a client or family member if they asked her to iron clothes.

All of the organisations offer companionship care. Clients who avail of companionship care will more than likely also request light housework and food preparation. Companionship tasks include reading to the client, organising post, watching television with the client or bringing the client for a walk or drive. Such companionship and/or supervisory care is often required for people suffering from dementia. One carer was of the impression that the social aspect of her job was often the most important. Another carer, who cares for a client with anxiety problems, explained that much of her time is spent calming the client and holding her hand. A carer who only works in a companionship capacity explained that in addition to light housework, she generally watches television and talks with her clients, and brings them for a coffee or a walk in a location chosen by the client. One director said it is their intention to employ persons over 65 specifically for this type of companionship role where, amongst other things, they would read to the client, organise post and help with additional home maintenance tasks such as gardening. However, such apparently "easy" tasks can be deceptively demanding in reality, with one carer voicing her frustration at the commonly held misperception that the job of a carer is an easy one:

The assumption is that you are sitting there with a cushion under your arse, with your feet up and eating grapes and watching TV. — Home Care Worker, Agency Mode

Five of the carers provided night-time care, while one provided live-in
care. There are usually two or three different levels of night-time work,
dependent on the care needs of the client. The five carers interviewed all
worked at the least demanding level, essentially being there for security
and reassurance, checking on the client once in the night. Live-in care on
the other hand involves working and living in the home of the care recipient for 24 hours per day for blocks of five days, two weeks, or one
month, although in some cases the work is split between two carers who
work day and night shifts, e.g. 8.00 a.m. to 8.00 p.m., 8.00 p.m. to 8.00
a.m. This type of work can yield a comparatively high salary for the
carer and hence, for some workers, live-in care is preferable. One director spoke of three carers travelling from Cavan and another from Water-
ford to provide live-in-care on a two weekly on/off basis. However, it
also has to be recognised that this kind of work carries a high price in
terms of personal freedom and flexibility. One of the care workers interviewed implied that she was effectively unable to leave the client's
house for more than a couple of hours a week.

The vignettes below give a preliminary insight into the typical work-
day of three private home carers. All names have been changed.

Vignette 1: Sarah's job

*Sarah looks after a lady in North County Dublin who is mobile
but had a stroke. She goes in at 8.00 p.m. and leaves at 2.00
p.m. the next day. From 2.00 p.m. to 8.00 p.m. the client has
some time to herself. They have a chat when Sarah arrives, she
puts drops in the client's eyes, if medication is due Sarah ensures that the client takes it, and at 9.30 p.m. she helps her to
bed. Sarah sleeps in another room but would check on the client during the night. In the morning Sarah gives her breakfast
in bed, once or twice a week she showers the client and
washes, dries and irons her clothes. She does light general
housework, but the client also has a cleaner. She goes to the
shop, drives her to the hairdresser, if she has a hospital ap-*

pointment they go together by cab. She prepares her lunch, they often cook together and she freezes a lot of the food. Sarah has been caring for this lady for a year.

Vignette 2: Jane's job

"My job is to put her to bed, and give her tablets which is very important, you have to keep them away, and I bathe her every Saturday or Sunday morning. I go from eight in the evening to half ten, I sit with her and I talk to her, and she watches television and then I get her clothes ready, and then I give her a sponge down cause she is incontinent and I get her ready for bed, I undress her, put on her nightdress and her pads, put her to bed and leave a glass of water beside her bed and then you lock up, put on the alarm and she is there on her own till the home help comes in the morning at ten o clock."

Vignette 3: Carol's job

As a live-in care worker, Carol's day begins at 8.00 a.m. She gives her client the nebuliser at 8.30 a.m. and prepares breakfast and gives her medication. Monday to Friday another care worker (probably a health care assistant from HSE) comes into the house to help the lady wash; at the weekends Carol does the washing. The lady then sits in her sitting room and has tea, says her prayers, reads the paper while Carol washes dishes, does the laundry and cleans the house. At 12.30 Carol gives the lady her nebuliser again and prepares lunch for 2.00 p.m. (Carol eats all her meals in the house free of charge; she does small-scale grocery shopping and the lady's children, about once a month, do a big shop). After lunch, she administers more medication to the lady. At 4.30 p.m. she begins cooking the dinner. At dinnertime she again administers the nebuliser and medicines. When asked where she learned these paramedical skills, she replied that another agency worker, a lady from the Philippines, had shown her how to do this.

Collaboration with the PHN and/or HCAs was noted by four of the carers. One mentioned that an Eastern Health Board carer (HCA) attended to two of her clients, bathing and administering medication. She explained that this HCA often leaves notes for the carers to update them on the health of the client and in some instances instructing them what to do. In addition this HCA also provided training on how to use new lifting equipment. Similarly, another carer noted that a HCA comes into the house of one of her clients to bathe her, however at weekends she does this work. Two carers stated that they work closely with the occupational therapists and the community nurses, however one carer lamented the fact that ironically in the wealthier areas this liaison is more infrequent, so older people are often worse off in real terms of care provision:

> Depending on the area, you could be working in a very rich area; you won't have the occupational therapist with the click of your finger, as they'll expect them to pay them. But if you're in a working class area, there is much more backup and facilities. In the inner city there're far more resources, in the suburbs you're on your own basically, you got to keep pushing we want this, we need this. — Home Care Worker, Agency Mode

Another carer acknowledged the importance of monitoring the clients on behalf of the PHN and stated that she tried to work as closely within the HSE regulations as possible. However, two carers were not satisfied with the level of support received from the district health nurses, with one stating that visits should not just be made when the person is in direst need.

Terms and Conditions of Employment

Employment Contracts

The home care market can be somewhat unstable, with staff availability and the amount of work available to staff fluctuating. For these reasons the ability to offer carers full-time contracts was seen as unviable by many of the directors interviewed. As Figure 6.8 illustrates, in five of the organisations all care staff work on a part-time basis, while in three of the organisations up to three-quarters of the staff work part time. Two of the organisations, however, stated that only 25 per cent of their staff work on a part-time basis. One of these organisations boasts a staff of almost 200 carers and 500 clients, indicating that larger providers with a regular demand for service may be in a better position to offer preferable working hours, terms and entitlements to their care staff. In addition to negotiating salaried contracts with a large proportion of the care staff, this provider has also offered a pension scheme to employees.

Figure 6.8: Percentage of Carers Employed on Part-time Basis

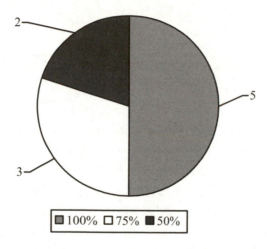

Corresponding to the part-time contracts of the carers are the lower number of hours typically worked by these employees. One organisation reported that the average carer only works between one and 10 hours weekly, six reported that carers typically work 10 to 20 hours weekly, two stated on average their workers work 20 to 30 hours weekly, while the carers in one organisation usually work more than 30 hours weekly (Figure 6.9).

Figure 6.9: Average Weekly Hours Worked by Carers

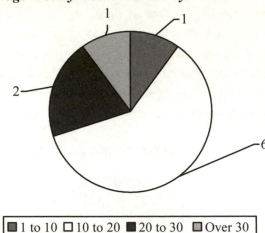

| ■ 1 to 10 | □ 10 to 20 | ■ 20 to 30 | □ Over 30 |

All of the 23 carers interviewed were employed on a part-time contract, however the number of hours they worked varied considerably (see Table 6.6). Seven carers could be classified as working traditional part-time hours, namely between 10 to 15 hours weekly, six carers worked between 24 and 45 hours weekly, while another six who were providing sleep-in care or live-in care also did not work hours typically classified as part-time. The majority of the carers indicated that they had the ability to dictate the number of hours they wanted to work, however due to the unpredictability of the health status of clients these hours may not always be constant. One non-Irish carer, who works 12 hours weekly, had requested more hours, but had been unsuccessful in this regard.

Table 6.6: Hours Worked by Carers Interviewed

Works Part-time Hours	8–9 hours a week	(Student) Only works weekends, hours variable	10 hours a week	12.5 hours a week	12 hours a week	6 hours a week	10 hours a week
Hours Equivalent to Full time Employment	30–40 hours weekly	30–40 hours weekly	Usually 24 hours weekly. Maximum 30	55 hours weekly	30 hours weekly	45 hours weekly	
Work Includes Live-in Care or Sleep-over	Sleep over three nights a week, 10.00 p.m. to 8.00 a.m.	50–60 hours weekly, day time work plus every second night sleep over	Sleep over, 9.00 p.m. to 6.00 a.m. daily	Live-in care three weeks on, three off	Sleep over plus day care, 8.00/10.00 p.m. – 2.00 p.m. Monday to Sunday	Presently only works mornings but soon to start night shifts	
Not Specified	Two not currently working	Not Specified has four clients	Variable two to three clients at any one time				

Rates of Pay

> The money we earn for doing this job is nothing to write home
> about . . . the hospital workers earn more money than home
> carers and you put in more in the home . . . with the agency I
> earn €8.54 an hour, if it's in the night €8.00, it's not good
> enough, for the same job in the nursing home they are earning
> €13.00 or €14.00 an hour. — Home Care Worker, Agency
> Mode

> When people feel valued they work far better and the only way
> you can make someone feel valued is by paying them more
> money. — Home Care Worker, Agency Mode

Wages across the ten private providers were relatively comparable, with
eight of the organisations paying carers between €8.00 to €10.00 an hour,
another paying €10.00 to €12.00 hourly and another between €12.00 to
€14.00 per hour (Figure 6.10). However, rates of pay are variable, in
many instances reflecting the duration of work, the level of need of the
client, and the day and time of work. Monday to Friday carries a set rate
while weekend work usually carries a premium of between €1.00 and
€1.50 an hour. Bank holidays (in some organisations) and Christmas also
carry a higher premium rate. Three of the directors mentioned that work
with high-dependency clients can attract a higher hourly rate; for example, carers delivering light companionship tasks earn marginally less than
those delivering care to clients with Alzheimer's disease. Rates of pay
can also relate to the number of hours worked; for example, in one organisation, carers get paid €21.75 for two-hour blocks, equalling €10.84
an hour. However, if more than the minimum two hours care are required, the rate of pay is reduced to €8.75 an hour. Similarly, workers
who only work a one hour shift (only available in two organisations) get
compensated for time and travel expenses; for example, in one organisation workers who typically earn €8.62 an hour, earn €12.43 for a one
hour shift.

  The rate of pay for sleep-over work is also dependent on the client's
level of need, with high dependency clients (requiring the carer to stay
awake) carrying a higher premium than low dependency clients who re-

quire a carer for the purpose of security and basic supervision. One carer reported a rate of €70 for companionship sleep-over and €90 for a high dependency sleep-over. Night-time rates of pay also differ between weekdays and weekends; for example, one worker explained that she earns €49 a night mid-week and €53 at weekends. Two types of options are available for live-in care: one in which the carer can avail of the client's food, or another where the carer brings their own food, the latter carries a higher premium. One carer, who takes the second option, explained that when she visits her clients she takes her own food, cutlery and bed linen. She was of the impression that carers who availed of the clients' food up to 10 years ago tended to be farmers' wives, but now are usually Eastern European. One of the non-Irish interviewees takes the former option of availing of her client's food. While the rates of pay are not strictly comparable between these two workers as they work for different organisations, the Irish worker earns up to €1,200 a week while the non-Irish worker currently earns €650.

Figure 6.10: Hourly Pay for Private Home Care Workers

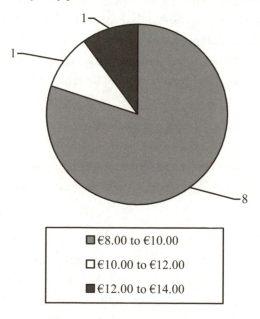

■	€8.00 to €10.00
□	€10.00 to €12.00
■	€12.00 to €14.00

Travel Expenses

> When they ring me up [to suggest a new client] I won't go to
> certain areas as the petrol is so expensive. — Home Care
> Worker, Agency Mode

Except when working on HSE care packages private sector carers are not
entitled to travel expenses. The distance travelled to clients is usually
entirely at the discretion of the carer. A number of carers stated they
would only consider clients within a certain distance or geographical
area. However, if demand is low and a carer wants to avail of work they
may have to travel a considerable distance. The option of working within
a certain geographical area may not be as available to less qualified or
non-Irish carers. One non-Irish carer spoke of a 1.5 hour journey for a
three-hour block of care. Another non-Irish worker living outside Dublin
explained that she often completes a three-hour round trip to deliver two
hours of care, while another living in West Dublin explained that she
typically has a 30 minute commute to her clients.

The advantages of working in a larger organisation also come into
play in relation to the geographical spread of clients. The four workers
employed within the largest home care organisation stated that their clients are usually close together and they are happy with the travel reimbursements arranged (i.e. travel reimbursements related to HSE home
care packages).

Sick Leave, Holiday Pay and Pension

> When we're sick the carer doesn't get paid, school holidays
> and stuff, you don't get paid. — Home Care Worker, Agency
> Mode

None of the 23 private sector carers interviewed are entitled to sick pay;
this is largely related to the fact they are employed on part-time contracts. A number of the carers intimated that if they do get sick they are
entitled to claim sick pay from social welfare (this group obviously com-
prises only those who pay PRSI themselves or via the employer).

Only carers paying PAYE (i.e. three in the company model and one
in the agency model) are entitled to holiday pay. Holiday pay is calcu-

lated on the basis of the number of hours worked. Carers working through the agency model are regarded as self-employed and thus not entitled to holiday pay. Reflecting the ambiguous relationship between client/carer/agency in the agency model is the following statement by one director in response to a question concerning carers' entitlement to sick leave and holiday pay:

> Holiday and sick pay is up to the discretion of the client, if they [the carer] are with them a long time, a lot of them [the clients] would give them something if they're going away for a few weeks, they would throw a few bob to them. — Director, Agency Mode

One organisation operating in the company mode has made efforts to offer a pension scheme (PRSA) to their care staff. This organisation arranged for a representative from a bank to visit their staff. The director explained that very few took up the offer, but this is something she regards as important and therefore in the future shall make further attempts to convince employees of its value.

Registering as Self-employed

> I would love to be legitimate as a self-employed person and pay my taxes but realistically it's impossible. — Home Care Worker, Agency Mode

Of the 23 carers interviewed, four were employed directly by the private home care organisation (company model), while the other 19 were regarded as self-employed (agency model). Within the agency model care staff are encouraged to register as self-employed. However, the extent to which carers register as self-employed is not recorded or monitored. One director reported that the carers' incomes are below the taxable income while another director intimated that many carers may be receiving social welfare and are almost always working part-time or may have other jobs elsewhere. One carer intimated that her employer is always very hesitant to disclose information on the names of her carers, as the director is aware that many are not registered as self-employed. The fact that care workers are not registered as self-employed means that their clients can not apply for tax relief on the cost of the home care they receive.

Among the carers interviewed only three of the agency staff registered themselves as self-employed. One carer who has declared herself as self-employed believed it was necessary, as many clients want to claim tax deductions, and she believed "you never know where your name will turn up [in tax audits]". She believed the "couple of hundred" she paid to the accountant was worth it and had the added advantage of allowing her to avail of certain travel allowances. Another stated that her husband takes care of her tax affairs but admitted that tax is not always paid "you know how it is; you get cash in hand . . . the temptation". One carer not registered as self-employed was amused at the notion that she should be self-employed when she earns just €9.00 an hour. Along with another carer this worker lamented that she was not employed by the agency directly and was therefore not entitled to the additional security such employment status offers.

Four of the interviewees employed through the company model preferred working within this system, having the rights of an employee, including entitlement to holiday pay (sick pay is not included as employment part-time). These carers explained how some of their colleagues are now working full-time on salaried contacts, however one carer believed this was largely dependent on the area of Dublin a carer resided in and the subsequent demand for care in that area. It was the belief of these four carers that the days of independent contracted home care were numbered. They believed the issue of insurance has become very important, with older people now in many instances asking the home carer about their insurance coverage.

Relationship with Clients

> Normally within the first two or three days you know what the relationship will be like. — Home Care Worker, Agency Mode

While one of the carers reported having eight clients, the majority of carers have one to four clients in any given period, with the length of this relationship ranging from a few hours to a number of years. Two of the carers interviewed mentioned working with the same client for three years, although this would seem to be an exception to the norm in the private sector. Two of the carers reported a high turnover of clients, for one carer this meant that in the six-month period of her employment she had six clients who had either died or gone into a nursing home. One carer explained that she views the new relationship as one which grows and is nurtured, until the passing away of the client;

> You walk into somebody and say till death do us part they don't realise . . . I'm with you till you die. — Home Care Worker, Agency Mode

Irrespective of the duration of the contract, however, by and large, relationships with the clients were described as close and companionate. Five of the carers compared their relationship with their clients as similar to that with a child, parent or grandparent, describing a mutual relationship of attachment and trust:

> People think it's an easy job, which it is in some ways, but it is important to have the right attitude . . . you need to think that this could be my Mum; you need to have that attitude to be a carer. — Home Care Worker, Agency Mode

> It's like they're another granny, when they get sick it's like it's one of your family is sick. — Home Care Worker, Company Mode

The length of time it takes to build up this relationship can vary. One carer explained that it took over a fortnight for the relationship between her and a particular client to warm a little. Another believed that some new clients are worried about their personal effects being touched. Two carers expanded upon the initial development of the relationship between carer and client; on first meeting, one carer believed it is important to be honest and put them at their ease:

> Elderly people can be very intimidated, very anxious very frightened, you have to put them at ease. . . . I'm only here to

help you, you're the boss, you tell me what you want me to do.
— Home Care Worker, Agency Mode

Another carer relayed the need to develop relationships by taking a slow, gentle and humorous approach. To relax her clients she engages in playful banter, holds and strokes the hands, uses humorous nicknames, asks questions and probes sensitively into family details.

The medical conditions of a client can in some instances introduce an element of difficulty in the communication process. One carer explained it is difficult to carry on a conversation with one of her clients with Dementia, as the client often forgets the topic of conversation mid-way and consequentially gets distressed. For this reason the carer believes it is better to keep conversation to a minimum. Another carer spoke of the fact that some of her clients have difficulty in understanding her and at times she has to take recourse to sign language. However, she stressed that she always tries to make the client comfortable:

> I have one lady with Alzheimer's and literally on a day to day basis you're a new person coming in, but you know by her that she knows you and she has built some sort of confidence in you. — Home Care Worker, Agency Mode

Various levels of professional distance were practised among the carers. While a number of the interviewees reported giving their telephone number in cases of emergency, to put a client at ease, or to schedule visits, others stressed the importance of maintaining a professional distance. Two carers stated that for some clients, the carer–client relationship is a business one with strictly no personal involvement. Another reported that she keeps the conversation professional and distant unless the client chooses to enter into a more informal relationship; she commented that:

> Some clients can't wait to see the back of you, and it's very professional, it's a business arrangement, they watch the clock, it's their personality as well . . . sometimes you don't mind spending extra time with the person, but you would with others, depends on the person. — Home Care Worker, Agency Mode

One carer (while keeping in contact with some ex-clients) stated that when working with a client she will not talk to them out of hours. It was her belief that clients should not get too attached or develop a relationship with their carers that oversteps the line. Contrasting with this perspective was the story relayed by one carer who suggested to a client suffering from panic attacks that she come to live with her. The client, amused at the offer, politely declined jesting that living in the carer's "mad house" with several children would drive her insane. Another carer noted that she tries not to get too close to clients, but she normally does, explaining that:

> When you are doing this type of work your heart rules your head. — Home Care Worker, Agency Mode

Private home carers can exercise an element of control in relation to who they deliver care to. If a carer is not happy with the relationship with a client, they can inform the company and ask to be placed with an alternative client. Five of the carers mentioned that they had taken such recourse previously. This ability to exercise an element of control over what clients they have is something which may be more pronounced in the private sector. However, the ability to switch clients (although not explored in detail) may also be related to the length of time in the company, the carer's previous skills and qualifications and past record with the company. For example, a non-Irish worker delivering live-in care was not happy with her employment arrangements, but due to the fact that she had just begun work with the company and had limited training, was not in a position to exercise such control over her work.

Job Satisfaction

Each of the carers interviewed was asked about levels of job satisfaction and what they considered the positive and negative aspects of their work.

Seven of the carers stated that the relationship which develops between them and their clients is the most fulfilling aspect of their job. Four carers expanded upon this; one noted that she likes hearing the interesting stories of the clients and their families; another stated that the positive relationship with her clients helps her cope when relatives are critical of her, and another two enjoyed the one-to-one aspect which enabled them to get to know their clients better.

Seven of the carers stated that satisfaction is largely derived from the knowledge that they are helping their clients. Two carers enjoyed the little things which improve the daily lives of their clients, such as cutting and polishing nails, applying makeup and washing hair. For another carer the knowledge that the client's family are happy with her work and that they can rely on her was a cause of great job satisfaction:

> In most cases they [family] treat you as someone who is coming into the family and they treat you as an extra member of the family, just someone who is a little more skilled . . . across the board you are never treated like someone who is the hired help. — Home Care Worker, Agency Mode

A sense of personal peace and enjoyment from helping clients was relayed by one carer, while another went so far as to say that there is nothing she won't do for older people as she loves giving them a sense of independence and pride, and remarked:

> I enjoy making people happy . . . the peace I have when I go to help them, I know when I'm going in I'm doing some good for this person, that's basically what I feel, I know when I'm leaving they are happy and they can't wait for me to come back. I know they are getting the full care they could possibly get, that's the enjoyment I get out of it, it's great it's just really rewarding. I know probably no-one would believe me but I love getting up to go to work, cause you're going in and helping someone you're making them happy. — Home Care Worker, Agency Mode

As well as being a rewarding job, the fact that a carer is essentially "their own boss" was seen by an interviewee as a distinct advantage of her job. She believed she could never work in a nursing home, as she "likes organising things and getting things done". She also enjoyed the variety of people that she gets to meet and believed she is good at dealing with people and meeting new people. Similarly, another carer stated that she enjoys her job as it is not as pressured as nursing home work and also allows her to have more time with her clients. The flexibility of the home care work is another unique aspect of the job which was cited by another carer as being one of the most positive aspects of her work.

One carer reported mixed levels of job satisfaction. For this carer job satisfaction is often dependent on whom she is looking after and the subsequent levels of appreciation shown by both the family and clients. On a number of occasions she has received "small little rewards", either from the family or from the clients, and stated that she values such tokens as an indication of the clients'/families' appreciation.

Negative Aspects of Home Care Work

A more diverse range of answers were given in relation to the negative aspects of private home care work, with some carers relaying negative facets of their daily work and others focusing beyond their daily work on the generic aspects of home care. Comments on the latter are closely related to the comments carers gave in response to improvements which could be made to the service and for the purpose of clarity have been incorporated into the section below entitled "improvements".

For four carers having to watch a client suffer, in pain or dying was regarded as the most difficult or negative aspect of their job. Sentiments relayed included:

> The worst part is when the person is sick or in pain. — Home Care Worker, Company Mode

and:

> I absolutely love every aspect of my job; there would be nothing else I could do. . . . I love working with the elderly. . . . I love every aspect of it looking after them unless they die, when they die then I hate my job and especially if they have a bad death, I would say to you I'm going to look for another job. — Home Care Worker, Agency Mode

and:

> When I see someone getting sick it affects me an awful lot, I
> tend to think about it an awful lot, I go home and I think about
> it and wonder if she will be all right tomorrow and the thought
> of finding them dead God forbid is my worst fear. — Home
> Care Worker, Agency Mode

Difficulties with clients' relatives were mentioned by seven carers, with
one carer stating she will deliver what the client requests rather than
what the family wants. One carer explained that this has taken the form
of clients and relatives unloading and sharing personal information with
her, another complained of some clients viewing her as a servant, while
another was of the belief that families paying privately are more demanding. The former carer also experienced sexual harassment by the
husband of one of her clients and complained that she is often asked to
do domestic chores for family members:

> The people I look after they all have families, and they have
> their own problems, so you're looking after the elderly and
> you're also a carer to the family. . . . You could be looking af-
> ter a man and he might have daughters and sons that don't get
> along . . . you'd have a lot of family issues to deal with . . . and
> they think cause you're there to look after Mam or Dad or
> Granddad you're there to look after them. — Home Care
> Worker, Company Mode

Three of the non-Irish carers had experienced tension with relatives.
Whether this tension is similar to that experienced by the Irish carers, or
has latent racist undertones, is hard to state definitively. One non-Irish
worker explained that she finds relatives very discouraging. She believes
they treat her like a housekeeper and are not polite to her and she believes that this is because she is black. While she can accept some racism
from clients who may be confused, she finds it difficult when relatives
verbally abuse and sexually harass her:

> The relatives make life so difficult for you, they make you feel
> like a nobody, they make you feel like you're a housekeeper,

> which is very, very bad . . . it can be very discouraging. —
> Home Care Worker, Agency Mode

This carer was of the opinion that the agency could provide more constructive support than they currently do. Similarly, another African woman also believed families are critical of her work which she also finds very discouraging. Another example of exploitation was mentioned by an African carer who delivers live-in care. This carer relayed how she asked the son of her client if it would be possible for her husband to visit for one hour a week so that she could spend some time with her baby. The son consulted his mother and they refused her this time off. Aside from the illegality of not permitting any time off, it must be questioned whether or not an Irish worker would be treated in the same way. On a more positive note, one African worker reported that except for one incident with an ill woman who later apologised, she had not experienced racism.

For two carers commuting between clients and traffic congestion were given as the disadvantages of their job.

Improvements to Private Home Care Services as Advocated by the Carers

> I don't believe it's down to any company; the government needs to open their eyes and see it costs less to keep them at home. — Home Care Worker, Agency Mode

> Every elderly person you meet their main fear is that they will have to go into a nursing home . . . remember these people were the guts of our country, they were the backbone of our country . . . give them their due . . . they should be treated like VIPs. — Home Care Worker, Company Mode

Grievances associated to the generic home care service largely related to lack of monitoring, training and inadequate allocation of resources and finances.

No policy of overall supervision was practised among the carers' organisations. Ironically, according to one carer monitoring within her organisation has decreased as the size of the company has increased. By and large it seemed "monitoring" was undertaken by the clients' family members, who would contact the agency should a problem arise. Many of the carers voiced their frustration at this system and called for a better infrastructure with a more rigorous monitoring system. One carer advocated the enforcement of rules as rigorous as those in hospitals.

Different suggestions were made on how to improve private home care monitoring. Since a primary motivation of private home care organisations is profit, one carer was sceptical that they would ever adequately monitor their services. It was her belief that monitoring should be done by the HSE. In her opinion the non-profit organisations were better at monitoring than the private sector organisations. Similarly, another carer believed the PHN would be the ideal person to supervise this work. This supervision would also be beneficial to the carers, safeguarding against harassment and exploitation of carers and guiding the use of hoists and technical equipment. Another carer believed the use of care charts and plans for clients (detailing the work of all those involved in the care package) may serve to improve service delivery. This chart would then be reviewed on a daily basis by a trained person. She also believed a strictly monitored clock-in-clock-out system should be enforced.

Five carers voiced frustration at the fact that abuse of the system, both by carers and home helps, goes on unchecked. These carers relayed stories of carers/home helps either not doing their work and/or not spending the allocated time with a client. One interviewee was aware of one carer who typically spends 15 minutes with a client instead of the stipulated two hours, and unless this client complains this abuse of the system will not be uncovered. These carers were aggrieved that there was no mechanism to make complaints to the health authorities which would enable them to discuss their experiences and observations of bad work practices. Four of these carers believed that improved communication channels among the carers and between carers and the agency may be one way to unearth this abuse. As one carer pointed out, a client may have six different carers at any point in time who rarely, if ever, meet each other. She contrasted this with her work as a health care assistant where she had frequent interaction with both the carers and the PHNs.

Since she began work with the private home care organisation six months prior to the interview she had not met anyone from the agency in person. According to four interviewees a meeting of carers every few months would facilitate discussions on workplace problems and also serve as a support mechanism to the carers.

For a further six carers training was an issue of contention. One believed training should be provided at least once a year to care staff. Another was critical of the current lackadaisical attitude of her organisation to training. It was her belief that training should be more than just manual handling and that an acknowledgment of the importance of interpersonal skills was needed. In her opinion many carers are insensitive and behave as if the older person is not there or is stupid, but older people are often "very vulnerable, don't complain, and accept everything as they are afraid the care will be taken away if they complain". Additional training on mental health issues and basic training in palliative care was called for by two carers, while another carer was aggrieved that she had to cover the cost of refresher training courses herself. The fact that training courses often train carers in certain tasks in pairs, which is not possible in the community (where carers usually work alone), was a bone of contention for one carer.

Ten carers were concerned about the lack of adequate financial support, information and equipment available to their clients. It was their impression that in some instances family members do not have sufficient finances and the home care packages do not sufficiently cover the clients' needs. Frustrations at the lack of provision of technical equipment, such as hoists for private home care clients, and practical services, such as occupational therapy or physiotherapy, were voiced by three carers:

> Sometimes I don't think there is much communication between some clients and the social worker departments, and PHN, at times it can be very hard for clients and you know they need a commode or hoist, and they are waiting, and the carers are trying to cope with people at home without a hoist, and that can be very frustrating. . . . In fairness though it doesn't happen as much as it did in the past. — Home Care Worker, Agency Mode

One carer called for more equal recognition of private home care organisations, perhaps helped by the creation of a central representation board. Inadequate nutrition, sometimes the consequence of family neglect, was raised by a carer, who commented that:

> The worst part is when there is abuse, I don't mean physical, maybe nutrition might not be great, the family might be neglecting them and you feel for them, and the elderly person might say why didn't they call, they said they would call. — Home Care Worker, Agency Mode

While a UK food delivery franchise currently offers frozen dinners from €4.50 to €6.50, this carer believes that many older people who lack access to Meals-on-Wheels have unhealthy eating habits. Another carer working with clients eligible for Meals-on-Wheels was disgusted at the fact that delivery was recently reduced from five days to three days. More psychiatric facilities within the community were called for by one carer, while another carer complained that older people are not adequately informed of their entitlements and are unable to avail of assistance in applying for them. In the absence of such assistance this carer said she often ends up being the information gatherer and co-ordinator for many of her clients. Relating to these grievances was the call by one carer for the government/health services to be more flexible and deal with every individual case on its own merits, so as to cater for the specific social and practical needs of each individual. Additional recreational amenities for older people were advocated by one carer:

> Down here there should be a meeting point for old people to go to, I know some don't want to leave their house but there are ones who would like to go out and meet others . . . entertainment-wise there is not enough for them. — Home Care Worker, Company Mode

Concluding Comments

This chapter on the private home care sector in Dublin is based on information obtained through in-depth interviews and a postal survey with the directors of 10 private home care providers and 23 in-depth interviews with carer workers in six of these organisations.

The private home care industry in Dublin currently operates in two modes, the agency and company mode, with the former being predominant. Within the company model, carers are employed directly by the private home care organisation giving them the rights of an employee and covering clients and employees alike under public liability insurance. While differences can exist within the agency model, by and large carers working within this mode are recommended to register as self-employed. The extent to which this is practiced is not monitored. Of the 19 agency staff interviewed, only three were registered as self-employed. Within the agency model, clients are typically told to extend their household insurance to cover the carer. The potentially litigious situations which could ensue as a result of lack of insurance cover warrants future attention and must be viewed as a serious disadvantage of the agency model as it currently functions in Ireland. A further disadvantage which can arise in the agency paradigm relates to the issue of tax relief, as carers' failure to register as self-employed means that private fee-paying clients cannot obtain tax relief on the costs of care received.

The size and future expansion plans of the ten organisations differed considerably, however in light of newly created publicly financed home care packages all were very confident of the further growth of the home care industry in Ireland. Indeed, two directors were so confident of this growth that they predicted that the private home care sector will ultimately surpass the non-profit organisations as the predominant provider of state-funded home care.

A distinctive feature of the private companies is that they can deliver 24 hour care, seven days a week. Another distinctive feature is the stipulation of minimum blocks of time. Costs for care can vary substantially depending on whether the provider operates in the agency or company mode, the minimum number of hours which may be purchased, and the care requirements of the person. Inconsistencies in relation to the charging of VAT also affect prices, and this subject needs further clarification. For all but two of the organisations, HSE home care packages were cited as becoming the main source of their clientele. Most of these clients were referred through hospital discharge planners or through the PHNs, which suggests these clients are more likely to be high-dependency clients. Somewhat worrying is the fact that the majority of these clients who are entitled to care package funding come via the hospitals. Unwittingly this may create a new perverse incentive to seek hospital care before entitlement to a "proper" home care package is obtained. Such a system which neglects the needs of lower-dependency or community-dwelling clients and fails to avert potential health complications is arguably flawed.

Newly-created publicly-purchased care packages are introducing new elements of competition amongst private home care providers. In light of these developments a number of providers called for increased regulation of the private home care industry. Calls for minimum training standards, specification of monitoring and supervision practises and fundamental changes in the operating of the agency model were voiced. Currently, great variance was detected in the training and monitoring practises of the ten organisations. While some organisations offer training, it is generally discretionary and in many instances at the expense of the carer. An increase in the regulation/accreditation of care organisations may jeopardise the viability of some of the smaller operations. Nevertheless, the importance of adequate documentation of supervision, monitoring and training must be recognised, particularly in the light of increases in publicly purchased but privately delivered home care.

The price of private home care varies considerably, from €26.93 per hour to €12.10 per hour. Fee-paying private home care recipients were not interviewed for the purposes of this project, however a future investigation of how, when and by whom private home care services are availed could yield valuable insights. The emergence of a "grey home care market" was noted by many of the directors interviewed and reflects the challenges families and older people face when trying to finance home care. The stipulation of minimum blocks of care by the private providers can be viewed as a notable disadvantage from the perspective of low-dependency fee-paying clients. Also of concern is the effect increased regulation of the sector will have on the costs of private home care. Increased regulation in the form of mandatory training and supervision will mean higher overheads for the organisations. If private home care costs increase as a result of such requirements it is probable that (in the absence of government subsidies and intervention) a parallel increase in the "grey home care market" will result, with people seeking out more affordable alternatives.

Private home carers are predominantly female, with varying levels of skills and experience. Recruitment of these workers does not seem to pose much difficulty, however increasingly recruitment of Irish staff was noted as becoming more difficult. While technically Garda vetting for prospective staff is available, the process is too lengthy and in the main written or verbal reference checks with previous employers are used. This practice cannot be viewed as sufficient and therefore warrants further attention.

Due to the unpredictability of the home care market, private home care organisations largely recruit staff on a part-time casual basis. However, increased demand (largely a consequence of increases in HSE home care packages) has meant that a number of the organisations are considering taking on a small number of full-time permanent salaried employees. For the majority of private sector workers, rates of pay are dependent on the day of week, duration of hours and the needs of the client. Carers are not entitled to compensation for travel costs unless dealing with HSE clients. Sick pay is largely availed of through Social Welfare (for those who have paid PRSI), while holiday pay is paid by four organisations. Private home carers usually work in a dual capacity delivering both domestic and personal care. However, the task of domestic care was viewed as secondary and is often left to the discretion of the carer. Sleep-overs and live-in care which can yield a relatively high weekly pay are also in the preserve of the private home care sector.

With a number of exceptions, relationships between carers and clients were generally close and companionate. Grievances with family members was noted by a number of carers, with perhaps the most noteworthy grievances voiced by the non-Irish carers. Latent exploitation and racism toward non-Irish workers was touched upon, with families requesting more domestic duties from these workers and not permitting adequate breaks. Whether these are isolated incidents of exploitation or widespread occurrences in the home care industry is something that merits further research. Carers generally voiced an ability to exercise an element of control over who they delivered care to and in what geographical area, however it seems this option may not be available to all private care workers, with previous training and experience and indeed nationality in some instances affecting freedom of choice. The carers also called for increased monitoring, training and supervision.

To conclude, the private home care sector has clearly become a part of the Irish care mix. With newly developed HSE partnerships the sector appears to be expanding at a fast pace. However, a considerable amount of uncertainty and lack of clarity exists about many operational aspects of the sector, such as training and monitoring requirements. Regulations and increased over-sight is required and must be enforced. In developing such regulations a number of key questions must be asked, namely: Is the state prepared to subsidise training of home care workers (private and non-profit)? What is adequate training? What are the respective roles of the State and home care providers in monitoring the work of the home carer? Finally the issue of who, why and how people acquire either HSE-funded private home care or privately-funded home care needs to be clarified. These issues and questions will be further discussed in Chapters 7 and 8.

Chapter 7

COMPARISON OF THE PUBLIC, PRIVATE AND NON-PROFIT SECTORS

Virpi Timonen and Martha Doyle

The three preceding chapters have introduced the reader to the central roles and characteristics of the public, private and non-profit sectors in the provision and financing of care in the homes of older persons. It should be evident that the three sectors differ from each other in crucial ways, but are nonetheless operating within the same social care regime and do therefore come into close contact with each other both at the systemic level and in the lives of the people who provide and receive the care.

This chapter will start by outlining the reasons for the importance of understanding the inter-linkages between the three "worlds" of formal care (and the "fourth" and "fifth" worlds of family and grey market informal care). The chapter will then proceed to examine the central differences of the sectors both structurally and from the workers' perspective. The possible emerging division of labour between the sectors and the impact of policy on the segmentation of care provision will be discussed. The chapter will conclude with an analysis of the possible complementarity of the three sectors in fulfilling their common stated aim, namely, the provision of quality care to older persons in their own homes.

Importance of Understanding the Inter-linkages

Understanding the connections, or lack thereof, between the different home care sectors is of utmost importance to the older person receiving care, the State that subsides or funds this care, the individuals and organisations providing the care, and to the functioning of the system as a whole. From the clients' perspective in particular, understanding and managing the inter-linkages between the three sectors is crucial. In some cases, a large number and variety of social care providers enter the home of an older person in need of care. It is to be expected that the number of providers entering and working in the homes of older persons will increase in the future as the number of older persons with care needs living in their own homes increases and as the "traditional" model of one informal carer working in isolation is eroded. The latter is occurring through forces such as the increased labour market participation of women, the greater availability and acceptability of formal care and public policies that support individuals to purchase care from outside the informal family network. Many myths about the disappearance of the family carer abound. While the purpose of this book has not been to engage with this complex issue, a recent comparative European study has shown that informal and formal care are indeed complementary, and that the latter does not crowd out the former (Motel-Klingebiel, Tesch-Roemer and von Kondratowitz, 2005). In the Irish context, an evaluation study by Timonen published in 2004 shows that for almost three-quarters of the recipients of the Irish home care grant, a full-time or near-full-time informal carer remains present. In short, the informal and formal providers increasingly operate in tandem and the presence of a formal provider does not "crowd out" informal providers. Rather, the two types of provider complement each other and constitute a stronger support infrastructure between them.[1]

The fifth possible care provider category consists of carers working in the informal economy, i.e. the grey market. In the light of the developments in social care regimes that share features with the Irish care re-

---

[1] It is worth noting, however, the apparent contradiction between policy emphasis on informal care on the one hand and the incentives and demand for labour market participation among the traditional carer cohort, i.e. women and older workers (Cullen, Delaney and Duff, 2004).

gime (such as the Mediterranean countries), it is not unreasonable to expect that this element of formal care provision will become more prominent in the Irish setting. The lack of clarity about entitlements to care
services, the comparatively high cost of private formal care services, the
uneven availability of services across the country and increasing purchasing power of families and older persons themselves may well push
the Irish care regime towards greater reliance on private arrangements
where a carer, often a non-Irish worker, is hired to work outside the tax
and social welfare network. Many of the individuals interviewed for this
study conveyed their strong impression that this kind of grey market in
care services for older people is already in existence in Ireland. While it
was not possible for us to examine in closer detail this segment of the
care services market, it doubtless contains the ingredients for another
extensive and important study.

Division of Labour between the Sectors?

Due to reasons outlined in Chapter 2, this study did not consult older
persons in receipt of domiciliary care services, and consequently it is not
possible to state authoritatively their preferences with regard to the presence of one or more carers in their home.[2] However, all other things being equal, it is not unreasonable to assume that the presence of one or a
small number of carers is preferable to a large number of carers, especially if the carers in the latter case are rather transient, i.e. working in
the care sector or for a particular client/employer for short periods. This
argument leads to the further deduction that it is more advantageous
from the client's point of view if care workers are trained and willing to
work in a dual role, i.e. to carry out both personal care and domestic
work. By and large, older persons with low dependency levels are likely
to want help with domestic work rather than with personal care and in
these cases a "home help" type care worker is more appropriate. However, it is likely that older persons who do have personal care needs will

---

[2] Indeed, despite the fact that HeSSOP I and HeSSOP II did make some inroads into
understanding older persons' care preferences, the fact (pointed out by Boyle, 1997 and
Pierce, 2006 among many others) still remains that older persons' own care preferences
remain under-researched and poorly understood.

also need at least some assistance with domestic work and in these cases the preference is likely to be for a "dual capacity" carer. Figure 7.1 below illustrates the approximate matching between levels of dependency and worker skills and capacities that is ideally made in accordance with the care recipient's needs. Note that the categories used here are rather rudimentary, and for illustrative purposes only: "low level of dependency" denotes need for assistance with Instrumental Activities of Daily Living (IADL) such as cleaning and cooking, and "interim-high care needs" refer to difficulties experienced in IADL and ADL (Activities of Daily Living) such as dressing and washing.

Figure 7.1: Care Needs and Appropriate Carers

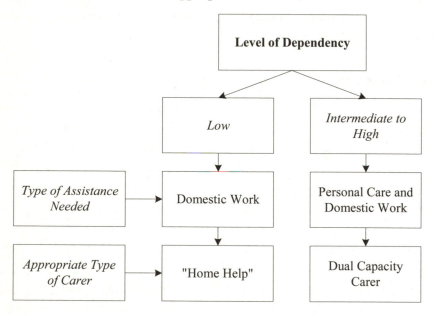

This means that while there is scope for specialising in the kind of domestic care work that low dependency clients typically need, it also makes sense to train a much larger cohort of home care workers who can and are willing to act in a dual capacity, i.e. to offer both personal care and help with domestic work. We will return to this discussion in Chapter 8 after a thorough analysis (in this chapter) of the areas where greatest differences between the sectors were anticipated, namely:

- Work tasks

- Terms and conditions of employment

- Recruitment pathways and the geographical spread of workers and clients

- Composition of the care workforce

- Motivations for entering care work

- Relationship between carers and clients from the carer's perspective.

By and large, the private sector was expected, *ex ante*, to require greater flexibility from its workers, especially with regard to combining the personal care and domestic help roles. Conversely, the work tasks were expected to be more clearly and narrowly defined in the public and non-profit sectors, where the terms and conditions of employment were expected to be better than in the private sector. The further expectations that flowed from the historical evolution of the home care sectors and its largely unregulated nature related to the more diverse nature of the private sector workforce, the motivations for entering the care worker role (some remnants of the originally voluntary nature of the non-profit sector were expected to be evident here) and the possibly more transient carer-client relationships in the private sector. The discussion below analyses the extent to which these expectations were confirmed or contradicted by the data collected in the course of this research.

Work Tasks

Table 7.1 below shows that the typical tasks, working times and number of clients do indeed vary between the three sectors. The general pattern here is towards greater variability and flexibility in the private sector, in contrast to the considerably more closely delineated tasks in the public sector. The work tasks performed by private sector workers were indeed found to be more diverse and more loosely defined, with greater flexibility in work tasks and working patterns expected from private sector workers. Job descriptions for the public sector workers are on the whole considerably more structured and clearly defined than for the private or non-profit sector care employees. While the non-profit sector traditionally provided (and in some areas continues to provide) only domestic care, noteworthy was the finding that almost half of the non-profit workers interviewed worked in a dual capacity, delivering both domestic and personal care. In many instances, their initial job contract did not delineate such responsibility; however as a consequence of both the deteriorating health of a client and the close relationship that ensued, an evolution into the role of personal carer often took place.

Table 7.1: Working Hours, Tasks and Number of Clients Across the Three Sectors

Care Sector and Worker	Public — Health Care Assistant	Private — Private Care Worker	Non-profit — Home Help
Typical Hours of Work	Typically ca. 20 hours per week, although some work up to 39 hours per week (daytime).	Great variation from 10 hours per week, to live in care for three consecutive weeks. Both day and night work.	Variable, but average of ca. 10-15 hours per week (daytime).
Typical Work Tasks	Personal care. Work tasks relatively clearly defined. Not allowed to perform any medical care. Majority of workers state that they never do any housework.	Mixture of personal care and domestic work, although some do specialise in one or the other. Many agencies also offer "companionship". Domestic care is usually regarded as an adjunct to the core service of either companionate care or personal care.	Predominantly domestic work (cleaning, shopping, errands) and companionship, although in practice line between housework and personal care often crossed. In some non-profit organisations a substantial number of carers work in "dual" capacity.
Typical Number and Type of Client	Usually 15-25, although can be as many as 30. People with personal care needs. Care typically delivered in short bursts of ca. 30 minutes.	Variable, typically a maximum of three to four clients, can be as little as a single client. Needs vary from extensive personal care to companionship.	Typically three to six clients, although can be as many as a dozen. Some clients only need domestic care, but many clients also receive personal care.

Typically a private sector carer works in two or three hour blocks with one or two clients per day: 15-20 hours per week is the average. However, a significant minority are engaged in 24-hour (live-in) care or work night-shifts or long hours during the daytime and evenings. This is in clear contrast to the public and non-profit sector workers who work comparatively short hours, in most cases during the day time (typically two to five hours during the morning and/or afternoon). The number of clients a private home care worker has at any one point in time can vary, usually ranging from one to four clients. In the public sector, personal care is delivered in short bursts of around 30 minutes to a large number of clients, whereas in the non-profit sector the average stay with a client is one hour, and the typical number of clients varies from between three and six.

More flexibility is required from private sector care workers than from their public/non-profit sector counterparts in terms of the range and combination of care duties. Whereas the public sector workers carry out personal care duties exclusively[3] and more that half of the non-profit sector workers interviewed focused only on domestic work (cleaning, shopping etc.), carers in the private sector are usually expected to combine personal and domestic care. Flexibility with regard to working times is also expected from (and offered to) the private sector care workers. One director of a private agency stated that night-time shifts are very popular among the care workers because many of them have children. During the day, the women look after the home and family but are free to work at night when their husbands/partners are at home.

An attractive feature of private sector care work is the insistence on the part of some agencies that care be delivered in minimum blocks of two to three hours. A care worker who had moved from the non-profit to the private sector stated that working in longer blocks is less stressful and gives an opportunity to engage socially with the client (naturally, this comes at a cost for the client and, outside the fully state-funded home care packages, would seem to be available only to wealthy clients). Many workers in the non-profit and public sectors viewed this ability to

---

[3] Health care assistants are structurally and historically linked to community nursing, which appears to enhance their self-perception and many of them are keen to portray themselves as para-medical workers and contrast this to the role of home helps.

spend longer than one hour with a single client as a luxury – in contrast, a non-profit sector home help organiser (manager) expressed the opinion that this would lead to a "waste of time". Some home helps expressed the wish for more paid companionship time, stating that home helps offer the companionship in many cases anyway (unpaid) and this should be formally recognised.

While most workers within the private sector can exercise choice regarding the "package" of work they put together, this is arguably the case for more skilled and qualified workers. Moreover, the flexibility expected of a private home care worker may also be a consequence of one's nationality. A number of non-Irish workers interviewed indicated that they cannot be too selective about the clients they take on. In some instances this may mean travelling a considerable distance for a two-hour care block. One non-Irish worker had been employed as a live-in carer living with the client for three consecutive weeks with minimum breaks. Two other non-Irish carers interviewed believed they have frequently been asked to do more than the expected duties of a normal carer and engage in a considerable amount of domestic work.

Terms and Conditions of Employment

Table 7.2 below summarises the key terms and conditions of care workers in the public, private and non-profit sectors. This summary indicates that the assumption of lower levels of remuneration and weaker social rights (pension, sick pay, etc.) in the private sector is correct. However, there is divergence within the private sector between providers who operate as an agency and those who function as a company. The terms and conditions of carers operating in the latter are preferable and more secure. Among the 19 agency care workers interviewed during this research only three were registered as self-employed. Carers working in the company mode on the other hand are employed directly by the home care provider. While their employment contract is also usually part-time, they do pay PRSI/PAYE, are insured by their organisation and are entitled to holiday pay.

Table 7.2: Terms and Conditions of Carers in the Three Sectors

Care Sector and Worker	Public — Health Care Assistant	Private — Private Care Worker	Non-profit — Home Help
Employer	Employed by a public sector subsidiary, managed by PHNs.	Two different types: "agencies" treat staff as self-employed, "companies" treat staff as direct employees.	Home help organisations: originally purely voluntary/charitable, now often limited companies with increasing structural resemblance to private sector companies.
Terms and Conditions in Brief	In principle similar to public sector employees; in practice implementation is inconsistent. €12.70 per hour highest point on salary scale. Little security in terms of duration, many on temporary contracts.	Rates of pay can vary considerably depending on time of day and care tasks. Average wages slightly above minimum wage (€8.00-€8.50 per hour). Poor social rights for those in agency mode (no sick leave, holiday pay). Those in company mode have slightly better rights (e.g. holiday pay). In most instances employed on temporary part-time contracts.	Pay and benefits increasingly similar to public sector workers'. Highest point on salary scale €14.60 per hour. However, no obligation to grant workers pensions and social security rights. Generally employed on temporary part-time contracts.
Unionisation	Majority members of SIPTU.	Unionisation rate close to 0%	Estimated 50% unionised (SIPTU).

On average, the pay in the private sector compares unfavourably with the hourly pay in the public and non-profit sectors. The typical hourly rate for a private home care worker is between €8.00 and €10.00. Rates of pay however are variable; some private sector providers grade the rates paid to carers according to the nature of the work so that more demanding care tasks and work during anti-social hours carry a higher pay. Some of the services offered by private sector companies require considerable flexibility and even self-denial from the care workers. Live-in work is the prime example of this. Live-in work can involve working and living in the home of the care recipient for 24 hours per day, seven days a week, sometimes with very few breaks. Aside from the sacrifice of personal freedom, live-in work tends to pay relatively well: pre-tax incomes of between €650 and €1,200 per week were cited by informants. In contrast, low-wage care (or other semi-skilled or unskilled) sector employment during regular working hours and within the 40 hours per week bracket yields only around €300-400 per week. Some of the agency directors acknowledged that some of the care workers complain about the low rate of pay, but also argued for the importance of keeping the service affordable to clients, even if it is at the cost of lower wages to the workers.

Many non-profit sector home care workers expressed satisfaction with the recent improvement in their wages. However, practices regarding social rights vary considerably between the non-profit organisations. Many do not offer holiday or sick pay, and have not implemented the recommendations regarding pension provisions. In the non-profit sector the typical entitlement to holiday pay is eight hours per 100 worked, although this is not always adhered to. Many of the non-profit sector workers interviewed were unclear about their entitlement to sick pay or pensions. Some home helps interviewed for this study stated that they had been offered PRSAs (Private Retirement Savings Accounts) but as these were entirely employee-financed, they were not seen as attractive, particularly for the older workers who would not have sufficient time to accumulate a pension in this way.

While the focus of discussion above has been on the home care workers, i.e. the workers who actually provide the care, it is important to note the pay and social security-related concerns raised by the non-profit organisers (managers) interviewed for this study. The salaries of home help managers is capped at a junior management level (ca. €44,000) on a scale used by the HSE. While their pay is based on civil service pay-scales, they are not for other relevant purposes considered public servants. Most importantly, they have no right to a pension, although in some areas the management committee of the organisation has made an effort to provide retiring organisers with a modest pension. Furthermore, in light of the very complex work tasks and responsibilities of several home help organisers their salary levels urgently need to be revised.

Both in the private and non-profit sectors, care work is characterised by precariousness. Due to the fact that the clients sometimes move into institutional care or pass away, a home care worker's working hours can fluctuate or, in extreme cases, they may have a short period of unemployment as they wait to be assigned a new client. There is no provision made in either the private or the non-profit sectors for occasions such as hospitalisation or death of a client. In these cases the manager/organiser usually attempts to stream new clients towards the worker as soon as possible, but this is not always possible and in such instances the worker experiences a fall in their income. One private sector company has taken a step towards remedying this problem by making some of its employees salaried. However, this move is more difficult for smaller organisations where demand for service can fluctuate rapidly.

Recruitment Pathways and the Geographical Spread of Workers and Clients

The labour market for private sector agencies is less localised than for the public and non-profit sector. Whereas the non-profit sector organisations recruit workers almost exclusively from their immediate surrounding areas, the private agencies tend to draw on a larger and more disparate geographical area both for their workers and for their clients. One non-profit manager, reflecting the perceptions of many of her colleagues, stressed that the "beauty of the home help service is that it has evolved to suit each area".

For most private agencies, advertising for care workers is not necessary as they receive a large number of applications from potential care workers, through their *Golden Pages* advertisement and through existing staff who refer their friends and acquaintances. Some providers however have experienced a difficulty in recruiting Irish staff and predict that with the expansion of the Irish home care workforce further recruitment difficulties of this group will continue.

The differences between the socio-economic statuses of the client base of the three sectors were not systematically reviewed. However, it is possible to make a tentative deduction that traditionally the backgrounds of the client groups in the for-profit and non-profit sectors vary substantially. Non-profit organisations were typically established to provide a service to vulnerable persons often living alone with limited community and family resources. For obvious reasons, the private sector does not have an incentive to target this end of the market. While the advent of publicly financed home care packages has changed the socio-economic characteristics of the private sector's client base in many instances, it could be argued that this sector still provides a disproportionate amount of care to higher income individuals. Though a number of the private agency managers operated a Dublin-wide service, many highlighted that their client base hails from the more affluent suburbs of south county Dublin. The corollary of this was the fact that the non-profit sector organisations are considerably more active in the mixed socio-economic environs of north county Dublin and the inner city.

Table 7.3: Recruitment Pathways and Geographical Spread of Workers in the Three Sectors

Care Sector and Worker	Public — Health Care Assistant	Private — Private Care Worker	Non-profit — Home Help
Recruitment Pathway	Formal recruitment channels in compliance with public service regulations. In practice often referrals via local connections.	Advertising in commercial media e.g. *Golden Pages*. Those seeking employment in this sector are often very pro-active in seeking out agencies and sending speculative applications. Word of mouth is also important.	Usually by word of mouth and connections in the local community.
Geographical Spread	Workers and clients drawn from the locality. Workers usually live within a short distance of client. Small travel allowances available to cover cost of travel where applicable.	Workers and clients in most cases drawn from a large area (often city-wide). Workers usually travel to work by bus or car. No travel allowances available except if working on HSE home care packages.	Workers and clients drawn from the locality. Workers usually live within a short walk of client. Some organisations offer travel allowances.

Composition and Management of the Care Workforce

The composition of the care workforce is more diverse in the private than in the public and non-profit sectors. The reasons for this lie in the more localised nature of the public and non-profit sector operations, and in the terms and conditions, both discussed above. Furthermore, the lack of regulation, particularly evident in the case of the private sector, also enables this sector to operate more flexibly with regard to qualifications and training, something which some operators take advantage of.

The population of home care workers is a heterogeneous one. While the proportion of females in the workforce is very similar across the three sectors (generally 95-100 per cent), the proportion of non-Irish workers varies greatly. The presence of non-Irish workers is currently slight in the public sector, somewhat higher in the non-profit sector and considerably higher in the private sector. The workforce of some private sector operators is almost entirely comprised of non-Irish staff. Agencies that employ large numbers of non-Irish workers tend to draw on workers from a fairly small number of countries: the countries that received most frequent mention were Poland, South Africa, Nigeria and the Philippines.

The age range is also fairly similar between the sectors, although the largest proportion of older workers is found in the non-profit sector. This is for the simple reason that this is the longest-established sector and also the least focused on personal care, hence in many instances being physically less demanding than care work in the private or public sectors. One non-profit organiser did however note that she would not "ask a 65 to 70 year old to carry a hoover up two flights of stairs." Similarly, one private sector organisation plans to actively recruit people over 65 for more "companionship"-type roles. Other groups that feature across the three sectors are lone parents for whom flexible and night-time work was preferable.

Practices regarding qualifications, training requirements, reference and security checks vary widely in the private and non-profit sectors. While all the private home care managers interviewed insisted that carers are required to have certain minimum training qualifications, the extent to which this is enforced was found to be dubious in some instances. Background checks are usually done through verbal reference checks with previous employers. However, the extent to which this can be done with non-Irish workers was raised by a number of managers. The vetting of prospective home care workers was practised by two providers who employ detectives for this purpose. While theoretically private home care providers are entitled to conduct Garda background checks on prospective clients, demand coupled with poor staffing means that in practise the length of time required to do these checks makes it impracticable.

In some instances the private sector care managers indicated that the workers are independent employees and should self-finance their own training. The principle of internalising the costs of initial training is in fact so ingrained among the workers targeting private sector employment that many non-Irish workers in particular undertake to complete and pay for (in some cases rather expensive) training courses before they approach the private sector companies. Several managers of private sector companies stated that they require prospective workers to do such a course before they can give them work. This can be seen as an attempt by the private sector manager to ensure a certain degree of quality among their workforce and therefore in the care work provided. However, in the absence of national accreditation, such training courses do not in any way act as guarantees of good quality care, and indeed it is possible that some dubious training companies have sprung up, incentivised by the requirement to present a "diploma" in elder care work.

Five of the ten private home care providers interviewed could be regarded as having standardised monitoring systems in place. In two organisations, the director makes monthly spot-checks on carers. In two other organisations a supervisor has been employed to solely concentrate on supervision of care workers, while in another organisation carers' clock in and out times are recorded on a computerised system which uses the client's home telephone.

Universal training requirements are not enforced in the non-profit sector either. Training requirements and stipulations were found to differ substantially among the various organisations. While a handful of the non-profit home help organisers agreed with their private counterparts that training should be self-financed, a number of the organisations provide either in-house or off-site training. In such instances selected staff are sent on specialised training courses, on issues such as palliative care, or complete basic training in first aid and manual handling. One organisation that places much emphasis on training has introduced a peer-mentor programme for its new home care workers.

Monitoring and supervision systems were quite informal in the non-profit sector. In most instances the quarterly (or once every three months) reassessment visit by the non-profit organiser served a dual purpose, whereby the organiser could both monitor the social and functional abilities of the client and review the work of the carer.

Arguably the public sector health care assistants are the most consistently trained workers across the three sectors. In addition to the almost mandatory requirement of previous training in manual handling and first aid, frequent refresher courses and additional specialist training courses are supplied free of charge to this cohort. Moreover, each of the LHOs where the interviewed assistants are based actively encourage their workers to avail of the eight week FETAC course, for which the LHO covers the cost. The PHN supervises the work of the health care assistants. Nonetheless, in all three sectors, improved monitoring of quality and standards is required, and any new regulations in this must cover all three sectors.

Table 7.4: Care Workforce Composition, Duration of Employment, Level of Training and Supervision in the Three Sectors

Care Sector and Worker	Public — Health Care Assistant	Private — Private Care Worker	Non-profit — Home Help
Female/male	95–100 % female.	95–100 % female.	95–100 % female. Male presence has diminished since systematic taxation of home helps' income.
Irish/Non-Irish Worker	Mostly Irish, with a very small non-Irish presence.	Varies across agencies, but considerably higher than in public/non-profit, some employ almost exclusively non-Irish workers.	Mostly Irish, with a small non-Irish worker presence.

Experience in Sector (Duration)	In most cases experience in either informal or formal care work.	Varies substantially. Some carers have long previous experience (e.g. in nursing homes), coupled with extensive training, others have no experience but have completed a short training course.	In many cases extensive, although many new carers have entered field after improvement in wages in 2001.
Formal Training	Fairly uniform levels of training required for entering role. Receive additional specialist training regularly for free without loss of income. An increasing number of health care assistants are FETAC trained.	Expected to have completed self-financed training or gained work experience before entering employment. Unwillingness of directors to finance this training.	Usually expected to have some prior experience of formal or informal care work. Availability of additional training varies between organisations, usually self-financed (loss of income while training).
Monitoring	Carried out by PHN.	Substantial difference in the monitoring procedures across the different providers. Half of the organisations interviewed have no monitoring system in place, the other half practice varying degrees of monitoring, from monthly spot-check to daily tracking of clock-in times.	No explicit monitoring procedures. Usually takes place quarterly or every three months during reassessment visits.

Motivations

There do not appear to be major differences between the sectors in the motivations for entering care work. While altruism may have played a considerably larger role in the non-profit sector in the past when the workers in this sector were genuine (unpaid) volunteers, the role of this motive in the balance is arguably no different from the public and private sectors at present. Indeed, as the discussion above has shown, the hourly pay for day-time work is at present highest in the non-profit sector. Among the 23 private home care workers interviewed, the stated reasons for entering the sector could be classified as practical, altruistic and financial. A desire to help and care for older persons was the stated motive for ten carers. The flexibility of the job was also an advantage particularly for those with children or those pursuing other jobs or study. For some private sector workers, the ability to earn a relatively high wage is an important attraction. As explained above, live-in work in particular attracts a wage that is far higher than that paid for similar work during regular day-time hours. It also appears very likely that in many cases private sector care workers who are liable to make arrangements for paying their taxes do not in fact do so. Understandably, the participants were reluctant to elaborate in detail on this point.

The home help organisers interviewed acknowledged that the pay for home care workers is relatively good, certainly in comparison with the rates in the past, and as a result it attracts more workers. In most areas organisers have a waiting list of people wanting to work. However, an interviewee stated that the improvement in pay "has done something to the service" and as a result "you now need to be more astute [about the people you hire]". The non-profit sector was characterised as "paid but still vocational" by one home help manager. Many workers in the non-profit sector entered employment when pay was very modest, and for this reason it is reasonable to assume that for this cohort of non-profit sector workers, considerations other than money must have played a significant role in their original decision to take up this role.

Many care workers, both in the private and non-profit sectors, have characteristics that lead to marginalisation in society and relegation to entry-level low-skilled jobs. In one agency, the majority of care workers are divorced; in another, the majority were lone mothers; in many private sector agencies the majority of workers are non-Irish workers, typically from either Eastern Europe or Africa. Some agencies tend to specialise in recruiting workers with shared characteristics. This might reflect their location in or near a deprived area or the comparatively low wages and undesirable working patterns that they offer.

Table 7.5: Motivations for Entering Care Work Across the Three Sectors

Care Sector and Worker	Public — Health Care Assistant	Private — Private Care Worker	Non-profit — Home Help
Central Reasons for Entering Care Work	Perception of health care assistant role as superior to other home care roles. Flexibility, altruism.	Practical (flexibility of work and financial), altruistic, change from nursing home work, financial.	Flexibility and considerable amount of control over hours. Pay perceived as relatively good.

Quality of the Carer-Client Relationship

"I have learned so much about life from them" — Non-profit Sector Care Worker

Several non-profit sector care workers characterised care work as a vocation, and described long-standing and close relationships with clients. The fact that many of the non-profit sector workers have been employed in the sector for as long as 20 to 30 years is likely to have a positive impact on the client-carer relationships, particularly as carers in this sector tend to operate within a geographically rather small area. According to one non-profit sector manager, "For many, [working as a home help] is a family tradition" with two or even three generations of the same family working as a home help. Many non-profit sector workers recounted examples of "going beyond the call of duty" (for instance, inviting clients to stay in their home over Christmas). This type of closeness is rarely evident in the private sector, although it is likely that the primary reasons for this are geographical distance and shorter duration of the relationship, rather than lack of affection.

A number of non-profit sector workers outlined that companionship was a very important part of their job as many of their clients are isolated or depressed and greatly anticipate the home help's visit. They all said they enjoyed their work, that it was challenging at times, especially when dealing with death, but that it was a rewarding job and the level of appreciation they often get makes it worthwhile. They felt it was rewarding because "you get back all you give", and many stated that the families of the older people valued their opinions and would often ask for advice. One woman explained how a family had asked her whether they should move their dying father into a hospice. The family followed the carer's recommendation that the man be allowed to remain at home. In addition to this type of advice, non-profit care workers often liaise closely with other key community care professionals, especially PHNs and general practitioners.

A number of the directors delivering domiciliary care in the private sector emphasised the importance of the quality of the carer-client relationship and claimed to invest considerable effort in this. Some private sector operators spend time establishing what type of person the client is and what type of carer they would like. The director of one private home care service believes that part of what they are selling is companionship, "particularly for ladies living alone". According to the director, the company pays a lot of attention to the matching of clients with the appropriate carer. The application form for carers is five pages long and contains information on the carer's hobbies, interests and the type of service they would like to give. This information is then cross-checked on the computer with potential clients to achieve a good match. Another director stressed the importance of hiring care workers who are "not nurses, not cleaners, but someone who is like a family member". However, such extensive attention to matching clients and carers is somewhat exceptional. Although all agencies and organisations in the non-profit sector stressed the importance of the right match, this was often arrived at on the basis of a telephone call or left to the discretion of the carer who paid the first visit to the client's home.

The quality of the client-carer relationship from the perspective of the private home care workers varied. Many of the care workers interviewed applied the standards of informal (family) care to their formal care work. The following statements by two private sector carers illustrate these sentiments:

> You need to think that this could be my mum . . . you need to have that attitude to be a carer.

> The majority of carers are not in the job for the money, cause
> in fairness it's not the best paid job in the world, a lot are there
> cause they really enjoy what they do and they know they are
> doing a really good job and the people are happy with them.

By and large the relationship described between client and the private home care workers was close and companionate, with five of the carers comparing their relationship to that with a parent or grandparent. Various levels of professional distance were practised amongst the carers, with some preferring to maintain a strictly business relationship, and others offering their home phone number and in one instance offering the client accommodation in her own house. Relationships with the client's family in some instances were more problematic, with families expecting the carer to take on additional domestic tasks and "get value for money". Similar patterns were identified in the non-profit sector.

Across the three sectors two themes were predominant in the interview material relating to the nature of the relationship between the carers and their clients, namely, great affection and sympathy on the one hand and the need to establish boundaries on the other. While at first thought appearing contradictory, most care workers are able to strike the delicate balance between retaining some "professional" distance and true dedication to the wellbeing of the older persons they care for. While the care workers had extremely high standards in terms of the quality of care and the relationship with the clients, they also frequently exercise considerable control over who they wish to look after, and have become skilled at drawing the line between care work and their personal space outside the care work. Many interviewees stated that they would never give their private telephone number to a client as this might lead to frequent calls outside the working hours, and misunderstandings on the part of the client.

Workers across the three sectors almost invariably stated that they love their work and get great satisfaction out of helping older persons to feel more comfortable in their home environment. Possibly because of their geographical proximity to the clients, the non-profit sector workers frequently performed small "neighbourly" services to their clients such as delivering the Sunday papers outside their working hours. Several workers from the public and non-profit sectors also stated that they had performed what could be seen as acts of extraordinary kindness to their clients outside working hours. These included visiting dying clients in hospitals (one home help recounted a story of how a client had died in her arms in a hospital, in the absence of any relatives or friends) and having clients as guests in their homes over holiday periods (two home helps recalled how one of them had a client over for Christmas Day and the other had hosted the client for St Stephen's Day). The fact that these acts of extraordinary kindness were most frequently recounted by home helps probably reflects their rootedness in the local community and the long-standing relationships that they often have an opportunity to build.

Many workers across the three sectors stated that the relationships with clients are not uni-directional, as one non-profit carer stated, "you get back all you give". Another home help stated that the clients are "just like your friends", while a home help with nearly three decades experience of care work stated: "I have learned so much about life from them [her clients]". Such sentiments were echoed by a private sector care worker who stated, "God rewards all good deeds", reflecting her belief that acts of kindness towards others will come back to those who perform them. Clearly the care workers often get much in return for their caring, and a relationship that gives joy to both parties is established.

Table 7.6: Perceived Client-Carer Relationship (from the Carer Perspective) Across the Three Sectors

Care Sector and Worker	Public — Health Care Assistant	Private — Private Care Worker	Non-profit — Home Help
Perceived Relationship	Relatively large number of clients and short duration of visits leaves less time for building relationships. Relationships nonetheless generally close and companionate.	Generally close and companionate. In some instances though professional and distant.	Many entered work before improvement in pay hence original motivation could be construed as largely non-monetary; also tend to work over longer periods, often with lower dependency clients in their own locality and hence more scope for developing relationships.

Conclusion: Different Providers, Common Mission?

This chapter investigated six possible differences between care provision
and care work in the public, non-profit and private sectors. The analysis
focused on (1) the work tasks performed by the carers; (2) the terms and
conditions of care workers; (3) the recruitment pathways and geographical spread of the care workforce; (4) composition of the care workforce;
(5) their motivations for entering care work; and (6) the quality of the
client-carer relationship, as perceived by the care workers.

The study was able to identify a number of important and policy-
relevant differences between public, non-profit and private sector care
work and workers. The three main differences relate to (1) social protection, (2) composition of the care staff and (3) flexibility in work tasks
and mobility. Of these salient differences, (1) and (3) have particularly
high policy relevance as social protection has a powerful impact on the
social security of care workers, and flexibility in work tasks and mobility
relates to the content and timing of services for clients. The central characteristics of care work and care workers in the three sectors are the following:

- In the **public sector**, the health care assistants tend to deliver personal care in short bursts of ca. 30 minutes, often visiting as many as
  four to six clients per day. Terms and conditions are good in comparison to the other two sectors, although the highest point in their
  salary scale compares unfavourably to highest hourly earnings in the
  non-profit sector.

- In the **non-profit sector**, home helps tend to spend a somewhat
  longer period of time with each client and in most cases have a small
  number of clients who receive predominantly domestic help and
  companionship service, but increasingly a combination of these and
  some personal care. Terms and conditions, especially pay, have improved significantly since 2000, but social rights are still poor.

- In the **private sector**, work profiles of carers show a lot of variance
  due to the fact that this sector offers the widest range of services and
  employment terms and conditions. Some private sector care workers
  are employed on a live-in basis (i.e. working practically 24 hours a

day for a single client); others have a larger number of clients (typically three to four) that they move between. Earnings potential varies significantly, but at the lower spectrum of earnings they compare unfavourably with the other two sectors. Social rights in most cases are non-existent.

It is also arguable that the three sectors are distinct in their niches and comparative advantages. While the non-profit sector specialises in providing domestic help and companionship, the public sector focuses on personal care (both predominantly during the day-time in slots of typically 30-60 minutes per client per day). The private sector is carving a niche in more flexible, dual role, night-time, round-the-clock but also companionship-type services. Live-in care work (at present offered only by the private sector) can be seen as having both attractive and unattractive features from the point of view of the care workers. The choice (where it is a genuine choice) to work as a live-in care can be construed as power to choose one's own work hours. Home helps in the non-profit sector also have considerable opportunity to choose their own hours, but the option of engaging in live-in care, night-time care work or otherwise irregular hours is not usually available to them.

While some differences in the motivations for entering care work and in the nature of the relationship between carers and clients could be identified, these two areas require further investigation through a larger number of interviews and participant observation with care workers and care recipients.

The results of this research show that the three sectors have evolved in somewhat different directions, and that in this sense there is an approximate division of labour between them. The different sectors have evolved to cater to different needs which are in turn reflected in the working patterns. This division of labour applies to two central aspects of care, namely the type of care provided and the patterns of care provision. One of the central questions that emerges concerns the issue of whether the three sectors should be encouraged and incentivised to converge, or whether it would be preferable to induce them to specialise further. The next chapter addresses some of the policy mechanisms that can be used to create more inter-linkages between the different providers (including a more level playing field between the different providers), the ways in which the care work sector can be made more attractive to employees, and the ways in which the quality and availability of home care can be enhanced.

Chapter 8

EVOLVING CARE POLICIES AND FUTURE DIRECTIONS

Virpi Timonen and Martha Doyle

This chapter contains a number of policy recommendations, or rather analysis of the changes that could be made in the Irish domiciliary care system with the view to ensuring greater availability of high-quality domiciliary care to all those who need and want such care.

The chapter addresses six inter-linked themes as shown in Figure 8.1.

Figure 8.1: Six Inter-linked Themes

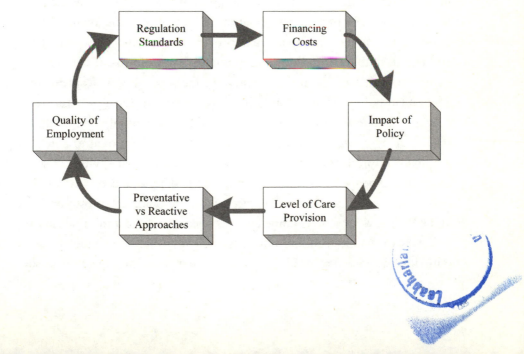

Strategic Direction: Preventative versus Reactive Policy

A basic distinction can be made in all areas of social policy (whether cash transfers or services) between preventative and reactive (or "curative") policies. In essence, preventative policies seek to impede the development of problems in the first place. From another area of social policy, examples of preventative policies are early education programmes that seek to ensure that children from disadvantaged backgrounds have a good chance of developing their cognitive abilities; and active labour market policies that seek to equip people with useful skills with the view to inserting them into the labour market. In the area of home care for older persons, the aim of preventative policies is two-fold. In the first instance, good home care can be seen as helping to prevent the need to enter different (institutional, medical/hospital) forms of care. Secondly, a highly proactive approach (such as adopted in Denmark for instance) takes initiative in consulting a very large segment of the older population (in the case of Denmark the 75+ population) with the view to assessing their care needs, and subsequent to this exercise, channelling home care services towards those who fulfil the qualifying criteria.

Level of Care Provision in the Home

While the more ambitious understanding of preventative policies (that involves screening the population as a whole to establish care needs) is yet to take root in Ireland, appreciation of the fact that the availability of good-quality home care can serve to prevent the need for more expensive and less desirable (from the client's point of view) forms of care has become very widespread in the country. In fact, the now widespread perception (in policy circles) that home care is a cheap form of care, while acting in favour of domiciliary care as a field, is potentially very dangerous, as the next section of this chapter argues. It is important to note that while the by-product of preventative policies can be cost-savings in some cases, the expense of preventative policies is determined by (a) whether opportunity costs, as well as direct costs of care, are taken into account and by (b) how ambitious home care policies are. If the aim of home care policy is to maintain in and return to their own home all older persons with low dependency needs, it is likely that cost savings will ensue.

However, if the aim of home care policy is more ambitious, i.e. to ensure that persons with *higher levels* of care needs can remain living in their homes, the costs of such care are likely to be higher than the costs achieved through economies of scale in institutional settings. Furthermore, if the opportunity costs of informal care are taken into account, care in the home is more expensive than care in nursing homes (but cheaper than care in hospital settings) (Hughes, Williams and Blackwell, 2005).

Currently home care services in Ireland are helpful in facilitating continued residence in their own homes for older people with relatively limited care needs *and* for those with more extensive care needs who have other supports, i.e. informal (family) care available. From the interviews carried out for this research, it is evident that more high dependency clients are remaining at or returning home with the help of the home care packages. However, due to the limited availability of these packages and community care services in general, residential care remains often the only option in cases where care needs are extensive and/or family support is lacking (for discussions on the underdeveloped nature of community care in Ireland, see Convery, 2001; O'Loughlin, 2005; Pierce, 2006).

This raises the following question: is it possible, within the Irish context, to increase service provision to the level where even persons with extensive care needs, and especially those who lack informal supports, can be facilitated to live in their own homes? Is the primary purpose of home care to react to high dependency cases or to try to prevent low dependency cases being admitted into institutional care? Ideally, home care would serve both purposes, i.e. be available to both people with low dependency needs and to those with high dependency needs who wish to remain living in their own home (while making allowance for the fact that in some cases institutional care may be the older person's own preference). Regardless of the choices that are made here, a national assessment system urgently needs to be put in place in order to ensure that older persons' needs are measured as objectively as possible. In the absence of such a national framework and guidelines on assessment, glaring disparities in access to services and the level of services designated will persist.

As Chapter 4 pointed out, the availability of home help services varies considerably between different LHO areas in Dublin. In the area with the lowest coverage, only 2 per cent of the older population receives home help, in contrast to the area with the highest coverage, where some 13 per cent receive home help. It is inconceivable that such differences would be due to radically divergent levels of need or interest among the older population. Rather, the lower levels of utilisation do palpably boil down to the lower levels of availability, which in turn can be traced back to poor planning. As Chapter 4 also pointed out, the average number of hours of home help received by recipients also varies considerably between the LHOs. Once again, this is hardly due to the fact that older persons in some areas need more help and support than older persons in other areas. Rather, the underlying cause is patchy availability.

Does Domiciliary Care Lead to Homes Being Turned into Mini-hospitals?

The concern was expressed by some of the interviewees that with the (welcome) promotion of home care, even for high-dependency individuals, homes would in many cases be turned into "mini-hospitals" with some unwelcome institutional features. It is necessary, however, to balance the slight negative aspects of bringing care into the home (e.g. the health and safety regulations that may require loose rugs to be removed from the floor) with the "greater good" of the ability to remain living in one's own home. The discussion on the financing of home care has already alluded to the fact that there can be (at least superficially) conflicts between the interests and likes of older persons and their carers. Compromises will be needed, especially with regard to arrangements that have implications for the health and safety of the care workers who enter the home. Most care workers are very mindful of the need to respect the care recipient's home. One non-profit sector worker with nearly 30 years' experience of working in the sector stated:

> . . . sometimes I would love to de-clutter a home, but they like it and you work around that.

Many other care workers across the three sectors expressed similar sentiments, reflecting the need for a compromise between the older person's needs and wishes and the care workers' understanding of the scope, nature and circumstances of their work.

None of the workers consulted in this study were officially allowed to perform any medical care tasks or even to administer medicines. In practice, however, all three categories of carer are sometimes involved in the administration of medicines and some para-medical care tasks. Knowledge of a client's medical condition is almost always known to the health care assistants but not necessarily to the home helps or private home carers. Many carers expressed frustration at the (ineffective and impractical) prohibition to perform any para-medical care tasks. If home care is to be made more widely available, especially to high-dependency clients, it will be necessary to equip more home care workers with para-medical training.

"Companionship" Services

At present, there is no explicit emphasis (in home care for older persons in general or in the context of home care packages specifically) on the social and companionship aspects of care. Whereas home care services for (younger) disabled persons often make allowance for leisure activities and "quality time", this is not the case for older persons who are receiving only personal and household care that is deemed strictly speaking "necessary": there are no "extras". However, in reality care workers are very often involved in this kind of social/companionship work, in many cases to an extent that is clearly beyond the call of duty.

Despite their clear willingness to provide companionship and even to perform altruistic acts of friendship, many interviewees suggested that there is room for voluntary organisations (and indeed individual volunteers) focused on providing companionship and covering the social needs of older persons. The wish was also expressed that carers (especially in the non-profit sector) should be paid for this type of companionship as "we provide it anyway". It appears that many carers in the private sector are already engaged in providing a "security and reassurance" service that can be construed as companionship, albeit in this case there is monetary reward for the time spent talking, watching television, going for a walk and similar social activities.

Impact of Policy on the Sectors

It is clear that all three sectors are directly and heavily influenced by government policies, despite the fact that such policies are often argued to be underdeveloped. In policy, the absence of clear regulation and rules is often as influential as the presence of a firm regulatory structure. When provider organisations are able to operate in a complete or partial "vacuum", they naturally diversify and establish their own procedures and protocols for areas such as staff qualifications and quality controls, and (as Chapter 6 on the private sector has shown), even in areas such as tax compliance, hiring and contractual practices, and insurance.

The clearest example of the impact of policy on the care services sector is constituted by the changes in the number, composition and behaviour of provider organisations since the introduction and expansion of the home care packages. The bulk of the discussion below relates to the issues that arise from the increasing use of this cash-for-care route and the resulting public-private partnerships, but much of the discussion is of direct relevance for the non-profit and state sectors, too, not in the least because *any coherent system of regulation and standards enforcement must embrace all three sectors if it is to function effectively.*

Choice of Provider

As the local health organisations of the HSE are operating with capped budgets they are unable to expand the "generic" services. Many of the LHO-level informants and home help organisers interviewed for this project stated that they would be keen to expand their services if additional funding was available.

Naturally, the choice can be made between expanding the "generic" services and making money available for provision of services by a mixture of private and non-profit organisations. While the former alternative represents the "service state" model, the latter relies on a public-private-(non-profit) partnership where the State finances services that are then provided by private and non-profit organisations.

Two very different kinds of actors are currently involved in choosing providers, namely the State (in the form of the HSE) on the one hand and individuals (and their families) on the other hand.

The HSE makes choices between providers in its capacity of a financer of care services. The HSE is given funds by the Department of Health and Children, and uses these to fund the services provided by public sector care workers (health care assistants), non-profit sector care workers (home helps) and private sector care workers. In the first and second cases, the LHO area in question does not usually exercise a great degree of choice as it is largely guided by past practice. However, in the case of home care packages the HSE does have choice as it can select either a private or non-profit provider or draw up a list of "approved providers". De facto, there is often little choice as the non-profit providers may not be in a position to offer out-of-hours services, and the number of private sector providers in the area may be very small, thus negating any attempts at competitive tendering.

Home care packages are currently delivered by non-profit and private agencies, and opinions regarding the desirability of private sector vis-à-vis non-profit providers vary among the LHO-level actors. In some areas greater use is made of private sector companies as they are believed to be the most flexible provider. Several private agency directors indicated that "increasingly business comes from [the home care] packages". The belief was expressed by some of the interviewees from the state and non-profit sectors that funding is being streamed into the home care packages and consequently into private sector companies at the expense of direct service provision, which in turn is being held at bay due to staff and expenditure ceilings in the public and non-profit sectors. In contrast, some other interviewees at the planning/financing level expressed their opinion that the private sector is the more nimble provider that is better suited to delivering the increasingly round-the-clock care that is required by some older persons with care needs, if they are to continue living in their own home. When the interviews probed into the reasons for using private sector providers (rather than non-profit providers), the interviewees at the LHO level justified this by referring to the "critical mass of resources", the more "professional" management of the private sector companies, their greater "flexibility", the "clear contracts" with care workers and the "quicker" processing of background checks.

However, LHO level interviewees in other areas expressed a very clear preference for working with non-profit home help organisations rather than private agencies, because these have insurance; established Garda check procedures; and closer ties and tried and tested working relationships with LHO personnel (i.e. better opportunities for the important inter-linkages that were discussed in the previous chapter). Other reasons for the preference for non-profit organisations were that they tend to be "locally grown and based" and therefore in some cases know the older population well. A further advantage is that long established financing systems and flows to non-profit organisations render the payment for the services more straightforward, whereas in the case of private providers new and often time-consuming invoicing systems have to be established.

While the home help organisers interviewed for this study would naturally not be without bias in their assessment of their organisations' strengths, their argument that non-profit organisations have "evolved to suit each area" is intuitively convincing. However, even in areas where non-profit organisations are in principle preferred, LHOs tend to use private agencies for covering those times and dates that the non-profit organisations cannot at present cover. In these cases there tends to be a strong preference for a particular agency or company that is perceived as more competent and compliant (with regard, for example, to insurance, training of care workers) than others.

The major procedural shortcoming at the moment is therefore the absence of genuine competitive tendering. Even where service level agreements are put in place, the absence of competitive tendering is a serious shortcoming as it can mean that the best provider is not necessarily appointed to deliver the services. With regard to these procedures, useful lessons could be drawn from both the UK and the Nordic countries where the purchaser-provider split is now well-established in many areas of social care. One such example of this is Denmark, where the concept of "free choice" was introduced in 2002. This new legislation meant that older people in Denmark could for the first time decide whether they wanted a private or public provider to deliver their home

care. Service level or regulated standards are specified by the municipal-
ity, and any provider that meets these requirements can offer their services (see Rostgaard, 2004 for further discussion). A similar system of
public or consumer-driven tendering operates in Germany's Long Term
Care Insurance programme.

Increased efficiency and responsiveness are unlikely outcomes in the
absence of competitive tendering procedures and quality controls. Introduction of transparent competitive tendering and independent quality
controls are reforms that urgently need to take place and that should lead
to a more level playing field where both non-profit and for-profit organisations can offer their services to older persons, provided that they fulfill
quality criteria and are competitive in the sense of meeting the requirements of the care recipients. While an LHO employee in charge of tendering out work may be entirely correct in their assessment of the pros
and cons of different providers, reliance on such impressionistic evidence is not adequate in a care regime where an increasing share of the
formal care work is being contracted out. The impressionistic evidence
regarding the comparative advantage of private companies and the al-
leged willingness of non-profit organisations to extend their services can
only be tested by leveling the playing field by opening the provision of
all or some (e.g. night-time, weekend) care services to all providers who
fulfill a quality criteria and are willing to be rigorously and independently inspected at regular intervals. The persons in need of services can
then select from among these providers the one that they believe best
meets their needs. A possible complement to such an arrangement may
be an expansion of public sector (heath care assistant) employment, although this is unlikely in the context of a welfare state/care regime that
has historically followed the subsidiarity principle and adopted an arm's
length approach to service delivery. A better way of ensuring access and
equity in such a "state pays, others provide" regime would be to approach the service user end of the spectrum, i.e. ensure access to services
to all who fulfill the needs criteria, however that is defined.

Financing and Cost-sharing

Charges

The issue of user fees is of little direct relevance for the State sector (health care assistants) or the private sector, as in the former no fees are imposed, and in the latter the client is either covered by the HSE care packages or pays all (or part) of the costs themselves. The policies regarding charging clients vary greatly between the non-profit organisations. While some ask for no contributions at all, others expect most clients to cover some or even the bulk of the costs of providing the service. This inconsistency in charging practices is in itself problematic. Why should personal care services provided by the State be completely free (in those geographical areas where such services are available), while the charges paid for home help vary significantly between areas? Furthermore, while the availability of home care packages in some areas is clearly welcome, it serves to further deepen the disparities in availability of formal care services between the areas covered and those that are yet to be brought within the remit of these packages.

As was pointed out above, there is considerable inconsistency in charging clients for the home help services. The non-profit sector home help organisers who had decided not to ask for contributions justified this in a number of different ways, for instance:

> We do not operate in very well-off areas.

> I don't go along with the argument that no matter how poor the client is they should pay [because otherwise they would not appreciate the service].

The organisers who had decided not to impose any charges also stressed that assessment of means is "messy", time-consuming and complicated, and therefore likely to be counter-productive. They also believed that many clients might turn down the services or not seek them if they have to pay charges — in other words that charges would suppress take-up of services:

> Old people and money is a big issue.

Other problems associated with charges include forgetfulness on the part of some clients. If payment is up to them it is not fair to the care workers particularly if they are paid directly by the clients.

It also appears that the granting of the medical card to all residents aged 70 or over has generated the impression among many older people that all home care services are within the remit of free services, which in turn means that these services are now regarded as more acceptable than in the past (c.f. the findings of HeSSOP I and II). While this (lessening of stigma attached to formal home care services) is in itself a positive development, it is nonetheless erroneous to believe that home care services are now genuinely universal in Ireland. As this research has shown, great differences persist in the availability of home care services, and in the cost of those services to individuals.

Some home help organisers who do ask for contributions justify this by arguing that people appreciate the service more if they have to pay for it. Furthermore, these interviewees believed that people are more likely to give up the service when they no longer need it if it carries a price (even a very low one). In most cases, the organisations that have decided to ask for contributions do this rather subtly and are prepared to be very flexible. One interviewee stated that the organisation would not ask for instance a terminally ill client for contributions. In some cases the decision to ask for contributions was made when a shortage of funds occurred and waiting lists began to build up. In the cases where charges were requested, these ranged from very minimal (a couple of euro per week) to as much as €10.00 per hour. In a small number of areas the home help organisers admitted to acting as conduits to clients who were willing to pay the rate requested by the home help for a fully private service, but this was an exception rather than the rule.

Some interviewees stated that older persons can be very reluctant to accept care workers into their homes for a variety of reasons. Concern about the costs of private home care is an important deterrent, and it appears that sometimes older persons are not told about the costs of care, which are then covered by relatives. However, it is highly likely that many older persons are foregoing care because of concerns about the high costs, and this is an issue that deserves careful consideration and calls for policies that would eliminate the fear of high costs.

In the interest of fairness and transparency, and in order to enable forward planning in budgeting, clear and simple guidelines on the extent of individual responsibility should be defined and communicated to the older population. Timonen (2006) has argued that a compromise between a universalist and means-tested system should be adopted in Ireland, where everyone is entitled to a certain basic amount of care (or funding towards care), regardless of means, and this is supplemented by a top-up for those on low incomes and lacking additional assets. The allocation of both the basic universal payment and the top-up would only take place after a socio-medical assessment has concluded that the person in question is in need of home care services. The advantages of the universal payment are that is it straightforward, clear and unbureaucratic, and as such would most likely come to enjoy great popular support. The advantages of the top-up are that it would channel resources to those most in need without stigmatising them (as the top-up would be part of the same subvention system), and would also help to control costs.

In all cases, it should be possible to use all or part of the subvention to reward an informal (family) carer, but not a paid carer who operates outside the tax and social security net. Consideration should be given to co-coordinating, or even fully integrating, the carer's allowance and benefit, and home care packages. Within the long-term care insurance system that was introduced in Germany in 1995, informal (family) carers are entitled to receive a cash support that is dependent on the level of care needs of the person they look after. This payment is not means-tested. The availability of long-term care benefits to informal carers in Germany reflects the belief that informal care is highly important, and desirable, and should be rewarded monetarily.

A tax-related issue raised by some agencies is that while people are entitled to tax relief when paying for home care services, up to a maximum of €50,000, this cut-off point does not apply when paying for nursing home or institutional care. Due to this discrepancy it may actually cost a person more to finance home care than to finance institutional care. In general, *the system of care provision and subsidies towards the costs of care should be designed so that it does not create incentives to seek institutional care instead of home care.* At present, the incentives are still weighted towards institutional care (National Economic and Social Forum, 2005).

Regulation and Standards

The considerable changes in the care services sector mean that there is a great need for regulation and national standards. The expectations of both care recipients and organisations financing care are changing, yet these expectations are in many cases not clearly spelled out, monitored or enforced. While regulation and monitoring of standards has to be considered from the point of view of covering all three sectors, these issues are most pertinent for the newest, i.e. the private, sector.

Taxation and Social Security

There seems to be considerable uncertainly about the liability of home care companies for value added tax (VAT). At present it appears that these companies are liable to pay VAT, although many of them do not. Practices regarding the taxation of private sector home care workers vary widely, too. Whereas the agency-type organisations treat them as self-employed (leaving the carers to make arrangements for their own tax and PRSI payments), the organisations operating in the company model treat the carers as employees and therefore pay their tax and PRSI upfront. From the point of view of both generating tax revenue and ensuring that the workers themselves benefit from being in the tax and social security net, the latter model should be encouraged. Paying PRSI would ensure that care workers are entitled to the employment-related disability and unemployment benefits. Occupational benefits, and pensions in particular, should also become part of the package offered to care workers.

Quality of Employment in the Care Sector

Social care employment in general suffers from being perceived as a low status job (Munday, 1996), and the lack of prospects and haphazard provision of training opportunities add to this problem. Currently the prospects for career progression within the care services sector are rather limited. Indeed, it is arguable that there are *dis*incentives for upgrading one's skills: despite the fact that health care assistants have arguably the highest levels of training, they have relatively poor wages. Home care workers need a career pathway, with promotion and progression prospects, so that they can at the outset look forward to a varied career that can evolve and lead into supervisory and management roles within this growing sector.

As previous chapters have highlighted, many home helps are now performing both personal and household care tasks and therefore are arguably engaged in increasingly demanding and diverse work. However, the same rates of pay apply regardless of the mixture of care tasks performed and it is possible that a person with a higher level of training and more demanding and strenuous care tasks is earning considerably less than a person carrying out light housework (although the better holiday and sick pay entitlements available to the health care assistants arguably go some way towards compensating for this). This is naturally not to argue that workers carrying out domestic tasks (assistance with instrumental activities of daily living) are not "worth" the money they are paid. On the contrary, the improvements in their wages are a very welcome development that should continue. The argument put forward here is that more incentives need to be given to individuals who are willing to increase and improve their skills, and to combine different work tasks ranging from personal to household care, as this combination is increasingly needed and is most rationally performed by a single care worker. However, as the complexity and diversity of the tasks carried out by home care workers increases, so does the need for careful monitoring of individuals who enter this line of work, and indeed of the quality of the ongoing care.

Most care workers are required to take the initiative themselves if they are to acquire new skills – in the private sector, in particular, the costs related to taking courses have to be borne by the carers. In combination with the low or non-existent monetary rewards for dual-role carers, this acts as a considerable disincentive to enhance one's skills. This disincentive should be removed with the help of funding the costs of upskilling and monetary reward in the form of higher wages for carers who are trained to deliver both domestic help and personal care.

Quality of Services

Any inspection regime that is developed and put into place in Ireland should embrace both the institutional and community care sectors, and within the latter, all types of services that are delivered in the older person's home, i.e. help with both activities of daily living and instrumental activities of daily living.

Quality of home care is an elusive issue, given the heterogeneity of the client group to whom it is delivered, their unique needs, social supports and personality characteristics, to name a but a few potential variables. While increased regulation of the home care market will ensure quality from a legal perspective (e.g. insurance and payment of PRSI, Garda checks of potential employees and ongoing monitoring of service delivery), quality on the ground as perceived by the home care recipient was not researched in this project. Rostgaard (2004), commenting on the Danish system of home care, which has recently introduced a purchaser/provider split, writes on the notion of quality from the recipient's point of view:

> When asked what quality of home care is to them [older people], this does not necessarily include more freedom to choose between providers. Instead, elderly tend to ask for more influence over the content of the care, i.e. freedom as to how the care need is met. They require freedom in their relationship with the home-helper; this includes being able to establish a social contact with the person, but often the home helper is under tight time constraints, or there is a frequent change of home helpers. Quality of care for the elderly is also the freedom to be able to themselves plan their day, and not having to wait for hours for their home help to arrive (p. 10).

While this statement relates to home care recipients in Denmark, it is highly probable that a number of these factors would be found to similarly influence perceived quality of home care in an Irish cohort. Focusing on home care at the provider level is essential for ensuring that legal requirements are enforced. Once these legal issues have been resolved, a bottom-up review of the Irish home care system is required to uncover older peoples' opinions on "quality" home care.

Issues of Specific Relevance for Home Care Packages

If the strong expansion of home care packages is to continue, it is of great importance to put them on a solid footing in terms of the assessment, qualifying criteria, quality controls and amounts of funding available. A number of issues arise:

1. Currently the majority of home care grant recipients originate from a hospital setting, i.e. they are awarded the package to facilitate their return home. Community-dwelling individuals are granted care packages, but the number of packages and the funding available to community-dwellers is lower than that available to those returning home from a hospital or other institutional care settings. This creates a perverse incentive for people to seek institutional care in the first instance, since a prior stay in an institutional setting seems to enhance the chances of getting a care package. The funding available through a care package should be based on *care needs* (and possibly to some extent on the applicant's income), not on the applicant's *location* in the community or in a hospital.

2. There is currently an array of programmes that seek to facilitate older persons with care needs to live in their own homes. Some of these programmes are means-tested, but others are not. It is not clear why this should be the case and the practice of means-testing for some programmes and not for others (when the aims of the programmes are similar) is unfair.

3. Currently contracts to carry out care packages work are awarded without proper tendering procedures. Service level agreements should always be put in place, and this should follow a process of *competitive* tendering. In order to maximise customer choice, the service users (home care package recipients) should then be able to choose from among the approved providers in their area (where necessary or desirable, with assistance from a family member or a health services employee equipped to give informed and impartial advice).

Conclusion

This chapter has discussed the main challenges that the Irish domiciliary care system faces. The pivotal issue is the regulation of services with the view to creating a level playing field that draws out the strengths of different providers and ensures greater degree of consumer direction and quality control.

Lastly, a note of caution about the dangers of excessive enthusiasm for domiciliary care: while it appears to be the preferred choice of the majority of older people, it should not become compulsory in the sense that no other alternatives are available. Security concerns and isolation in fast-changing neighbourhoods may mean that care in the home is no longer the preferred choice for some older persons. In these cases, the stigma associated with assisted living and institutional care settings can cause unnecessary distress for the person who may wish to move away from home. One central aim of care policies for the older population should always be genuine choice, and this can only exist where *a range of high quality care options* are available.

Chapter 9

CONCLUSION

Virpi Timonen

Why is Home Care So Important?

The practical and policy importance of domiciliary care for older persons cannot be over-stated. In fact, given its salience for the well-being and autonomy of ageing populations, the nurturing and fostering of inter-generational and community relationships, and for the economy and the labour market, it is not an exaggeration to say that the home care of older persons is among the most pivotal issues facing societies and policy makers today.

Chapter 1 of this book set out the complex care mix that exists in Ire-land, consisting of predominantly informal (family) care but also pub-licly and privately financed and provided formal care services. It has been remarked that "[social care services] are a barometer of the balance of the public and private worlds within a society" (Sipilä, Anttonen and Baldock, 2003, p. 2). Many individuals and policy-makers in Ireland have a firm belief in the primacy of informal care, and encouraging this form of care with the help of means-tested subvention payments to fam-ily carers was the keystone of Irish care policy for a long time, and still remains an important component (Yeates, 1997; Timonen and McMenamin, 2002). However, even the staunchest advocates of the pre-eminence of informal care are in most cases prepared to admit that policy interventions from outside the family and immediate community circles should be developed and deployed in order to ensure that some formal care is available for those with no family, or only distant family members, and to relieve family care-givers' stress. In other words, while the *extent* and *nature* of policy interventions in the domiciliary care of older persons are subjects of often passionate debate that impinges on our ideas of the proper spheres of public and private responsibility, there is consensus over the desirability of *some* policy interventions in this area.

Furthermore, within the sphere of formal care provision, the proper sources of finance and care delivery are subjects of debate that often leads back to broader political preferences and conceptualisation of the desirability of public and private sector involvement in the provision of services. While those on the centre-right tend to favour private sector companies as providers of home care, those on the centre-left have a preference for the public sector. In the area of financing, those towards the left of the political spectrum advocate public responsibility for the costs of care, while those with more right-leaning sympathies incline towards private responsibility for the costs of care. All social care systems embody implicit or explicit judgments on the appropriate extent of public and private responsibility for the costs of care. In the Irish case, these are implicit, often only vaguely spelled out and inconsistently applied. Nonetheless, there can be little doubt that in Ireland, families and individuals are in most cases expected to cover the bulk of the costs of care, whether indirectly (in the form of the opportunity costs incurred by informal carers) or directly (in the form of fees paid for [private] nursing home care and other care services delivered by paid outsiders). In the light of this assumed and de facto family responsibility, the organisation and financing of (home) care services is an issue that concerns the young and the old alike.

Purpose and Remit of this Study

This book has not sought to engage in the complex moral and value debates surrounding the appropriate division of labour between the public and private spheres, whether in the financing or the provision of care for older persons in their own homes. Rather, we have sought to map out the situation as regards the formal provision of home care services to older people in Dublin, which to a considerable degree also reflects the evolving home care situation in the rest of the country. This provided us with the ideal case study for analysing the respective roles and interaction of the public, private and non-profit sectors. While we have not examined the informal care sector *per se* (this will be the subject of future research), given the centrality of family care in this country, it is clearly not possible to study formal care without in the process extracting some information on the informal sphere of caregiving. Indeed, many of our interviewees who are involved in the delivery of formal care to older persons made references to their interactions (or, poignantly, lack thereof) with family members. From previous research (Timonen, 2004) we know that even among those who receive significant amounts of formal care, informal carers are in most cases the key individuals who underpin and co-ordinate the often complex care arrangements, and indeed continue to make very considerable inputs after the introduction of formal care. Research conducted in other care regimes, too, has shown that the relationship between formal and informal care is not zero-sum in nature: rather than crowding each other out, the two complement each other (Motel-Klingebiel, Tesch-Roemer and von Kondratowitz, 2005).

This research project engaged in the painting of a clear and up-to-date picture of formal home care services, because the information and analysis that were to result from this exercise would be of value to all sides in the debate and the entire range of actors who are involved in financing, providing, planning, analysing and evaluating home care services. In short, this research does not seek to endorse or reject any particular model of home care provision. Rather, the intention has been to highlight the characteristics of the public, private and non-profit sectors as they engage in the highly complex tasks involved in the process of formal home care provision. Whether our findings, analysis and recommendations are taken on board by actors involved in formal care planning and provision is naturally largely outside our control. However, regardless of the direction that policy will take, the time is now ripe for spelling out more clearly the delineations between public and private responsibility, both in financing and delivering home care in Ireland, and only when this task has been completed can the ageing population of Ireland plan and arrange for the eventuality of their care needs in an informed manner. At present, the task of planning, organising and financing care is often made very difficult and stressful due not so to much the lack of information as the lack of clear, transparent and consistently applied guidelines and assessments and the patchiness of service provision across the country. The bewildering mixture of exhortations to take responsibility within families and the sporadic availability of formal services/cash-for-care serves continue to create uncertainty among many people who perceive the formal structure of entitlements as inconsistent and unfair. Remedying this situation by defining clearly the limits of public and private responsibility in the area of long-term care for older persons should be an urgent policy priority.

Rootedness in History, Impact of New Policy

As Chapter 3 of this book has highlighted, domiciliary care systems are in all cases a result of historical evolution, which reflects the Church-State and Centre-Periphery relations and dynamics (Alber, 1995). In the case of Ireland, the Church and the voluntary sector broadly defined have historically played a more dominant role than the State in the development of the domiciliary care services sector. The organisation of community care services was rooted in Catholic social thinking and the subsidiarity principle, which dictates that the State should only intervene when first and second order actors (families, community and voluntary organisations) have failed in their mission to organise care for the frail older members of society. For a long time, this emphasis on familialism and subsidiarity served to prevent an increase in the role of the State in financing and providing community care (although, as Chapter 3 showed, the State's role was considerable in both financing and providing institutional care). Calls to clarify the role and responsibility of the public (health) authorities in relation to the provision and monitoring of domiciliary care have been advanced for more than 25 years. The roles of both the State and the non-profit and private sectors in the domiciliary care of older persons have undergone dramatic change in the past decade, and this project set out to understand the causes, consequences and nature of this change.

With the view to understanding the changing interplay of the public, private and non-profit sectors in the home care of older persons, we interviewed 125 individuals within organisations involved in the financing and delivery of home care, including 63 home care workers from the three sectors. While the Irish state has consistently avoided becoming extensively involved in the *provision* of care, it has expanded its role in *financing* care provided by other actors, initially by the non-profit (mostly religious) organisations and more recently private sector companies. From the mid-1970s to the present this funding has been made on a discretionary basis by service level agreements as opposed to contractual agreements which are more formal and binding. Chapter 4 analysed the shift towards greater public sector involvement in the financing of care (and to a limited extent the provision of care); Chapter 5 mapped out the changes in the non-profit sector; and Chapter 6 analysed the novel phenomenon of private sector companies specialising in the non-medical home care of older persons. These three chapters, and the comparative discussion that followed in Chapters 7 and 8, analysed the impact of the new cash-for-care programme (home care grants/packages), and made comparisons between the nature of services and quality of employment offered by the public, private and non-profit sectors.

Positive and Negative Aspects of Current System

This book has argued that all three sectors, the public, private and non-profit, have played an important role in the (ongoing) evolution of domiciliary care for older persons in Ireland. The non-profit sector is the longest-established of the three sectors and continues to be predominant in terms of hours of care provided. However, the sector has undergone extensive changes and is arguably under pressure in the face of an increasing non-profit/private sector mix in the provision of care. This mix in turn can be partly traced back to the introduction of cash-for-care (home care packages) that can be used to hire either private or non-profit sector carers, and increasingly the former. The impact of cash-for-care is a good illustration of the far-reaching consequences of the apparently distanced relationship of the State to home care provision. While cash-for-care allows the State to expand its role in the financing of care "at arm's length", in practice this policy of channelling funds to providers has contributed very significantly to a dramatic change in the make-up of home care provision in Ireland.

This book has also argued that there are some signs of an emerging distribution of labour between the three sectors involved in the domiciliary care of older persons. While companionship care is an important component in the work of all home care workers (regardless of whether they are employed by public, private or non-profit organisations), this type of care is arguably a more prominent part of the work carried out by the non-profit sector workers, and to some extent also of the private sector services (although this seems to depend somewhat on whether the care is privately or publicly financed). The public sector care workers (health care assistants) are predominantly focused on personal care, delivered in short bursts. By contrast, non-profit sector workers (home helps) are first and foremost engaged in domestic care tasks, although, again, in practice it is often impossible to separate them from some degree of personal care. Moreover, in certain areas a "professionalisation" of the non-profit sector has occurred, with many home helps up-skilling themselves, and thereby transforming the role of traditional domestic helper into that of a carer providing both personal care and home help as traditionally understood.

In terms of the working patterns, private sector workers are more likely than their public and non-profit sector counterparts to work irregular and longer hours, including night-time work. This flexibility is often referred to by those who believe in the superiority of the private sector as service provider. However, it is likely that, given additional funding, the non-profit and public sectors would be able and willing to provide more flexible and out-of-hours services also. Furthermore, the terms and conditions of care workers in the private sector are in most cases less desirable than those in the public and non-profit sectors (with some of our interviewees quoting very low hourly wages), although the flexibility and in some cases greater earnings potential allowed by longer and more anti-social hours are arguably important pull-factors that attract workers to the private sector. The presence of non-Irish care workers is at present notable in the private home care sector and the "grey home care market". Experiences of exploitation and racism by non-Irish workers were alluded to in the course of a number of interviews; these may go on unchecked if adequate safeguards are not put in place.

Some of the negative aspects of the current home care system in Ireland have already been highlighted above, namely the lack of clarity and consistency regarding entitlements and the respective responsibilities of the state and individuals. This in turn makes it difficult for individuals to plan their own or family members' care in a rational way and also makes it difficult for provider organisations to project their future activity levels and revenues. It is impossible to predict how the care mix in Ireland will evolve in the future. However, assuming that the state expands its role in financing home care but remains reluctant to increase its efforts in the area of direct public service provision (a reasonable assumption in the light of developments to date), and also assuming that increasing numbers of older persons with varying degrees of care needs are to be enabled to live in their own homes, the role of the private sector in the provision of home care services is likely to expand strongly in the future.

This means that regulation and monitoring of all providers is of great importance. The State is accountable for the public resources it spends in (part) financing care delivered by other providers, which entails responsibility for ensuring that the services hired with the help of public monies are of good standard and delivered by trained care givers who are adequately monitored and also properly remunerated, taxed and insured for the work that they carry out. The issue of training, monitoring and supervision of domiciliary care is of fundamental importance. Even if the State ultimately assumes a distant role in the delivery of domiciliary care, it will have to assume responsibility for the enforcement of minimum training and supervisory standards among the service providers it subcontracts care to. The specification and enforcement of these standards are not easy tasks. Adequate supervision and quality control involves the creation of an independent inspectorate, tasked with regulating and monitoring all three provider sectors and all forms of home care (personal care and domestic help). Training and qualifications are important components of quality control. Mandatory training will doubtless only be taken up if subsidised or enforced by the State, and this in turn will have implications for the recruitment of care workers and cost of services. Nonetheless, ignoring the duties of ensuring quality care to care recipients and ensuring good terms and conditions of employment for care workers would be grave errors that would sooner or later result in abuses of various kinds. It is also worth bearing in mind (c.f. Chapter 3 on the historical background) that such monitoring of quality is in perfect accord with one central aspect of the subsidiarity principle as outlined in *Quadragesima Anno* (Pope Pius XI, 1931, § 79, 80):

> The State . . . alone can effectively accomplish these: direct-ing, watching, stimulating, restraining, as circumstances sug-gest and necessity demands. [emphasis added]

In addition to clarity regarding entitlements and regulation with the view to ensuring the quality of services, other important issues from the ser-vice users' perspective are the extent of co-financing required and the co-ordination of the various (formal and informal) carers. The research conducted for this study revealed a range of attitudes towards the issue of co-financing, ranging from endorsement of extensive co-payments (es-pecially in the case of wealthier older persons/families) to the conviction that the services should be universally available to all on the basis of need alone, in the absence of any charges. While universal access to free services is in principle the most desirable option, this is unlikely in the context of a low-tax/low-spend welfare state such as Ireland. In the ab-sence of provision that would meet demand, the likely outcome would be a bifurcation of the care system into the "free" services sector used by those with the skills to access services under the circumstances of inade-quate supply and the "paid" services sector accessed by those with suffi-cient purchasing power, with many individuals in genuine need lacking access to adequate services. A system which only supports the abject poor (such as that in existence in the United States) is not desirable and ultimately will not solve any of the current woes relating to the health and social care of older people. Arguably, such a tightly means-tested system would mean that a large proportion of those in the "middle strata of society" will do without, the illegal grey care market will expand, care-giver burden will rise and many older people will not be able to age with the dignity they deserve.

In the Irish context, possibly the most equitable, realistic and sustain-able alternative would be to make a basic amount of services and/or financing universal, and to make the remaining services/funding income-dependent. This would ensure that all older persons with care needs (as defined and assessed with the help of national assessment protocols) would be able to access some services/funding, from a basic minima to full coverage, which in turn would help to ensure the popular support and therefore the long-term sustainability of the system. Our study did not engage in detail in the complex questions surrounding financing, but in the absence of a strong social insurance tradition in Ireland, it appears most logical and acceptable to fund such entitlements out of general tax revenue (for a more detailed discussion on this, see Timonen, 2006).

The co-ordination tasks can be very complex in a system that relies on a variety of providers, as the total number of (formal and informal) carers involved in the care of an older person can be as high as six to eight (e.g. for an individual requiring 24-hour supervision, personal and medical care and help with domestic work). While the presence of an informal carer is often decisive in successfully undertaking this co-ordination task, the interviews we carried out showed that in some cases the care workers also liaise with other formal service providers (GPs, PHNs, other home carers) and thus voluntarily carry out this often complex task. PHNs and home help organisers also sometimes act as coordinators, but practices and levels of involvement vary, and in some areas there is very little communication or co-ordination. Regardless of future changes in the balance between public, private and non-profit sectors on the one hand and the informal and formal carers on the other hand, the task of coordinating the providers will remain a crucial one as it is unlikely that the majority of older persons with care needs will in the future have only one carer.

"Policy Learning" from Other Countries

Transplanting home care policies from one care system to another is naturally not possible, or desirable. However, an understanding of how home care services are organised in other countries can be very valuable in gaining a better understanding of the unique features of the Irish setting, and the aspects of home care systems that have positive and negative impacts. For instance, research in France has revealed that the condition of posthumous asset recovery in the PSD (Prestation Spécifique Dépendence) long-term care funding scheme drove down take-up rates of care services for older people. Subsequently, the requirement that part of costs be recouped from the deceased beneficiary's estate was abolished in the new APA (Allocation Personnalisée d'Autonomie) system. In the light of such examples, it would be unfortunate if similar experiments were conducted in Ireland, only to discover that they drive down take-up of services, even where badly needed. This would be the most harmful consequence that a (home) care policy could have from the point of view of those who need the services. On the other hand, as Chapter 8 highlighted, a number of countries (e.g. Denmark, Netherlands) have adopted consumer-led systems of community care provision that could well yield themselves to adaptation in the Irish context.

Ways Forward

The task of mapping out formal care provision is a very complex but interesting and important one. For all its shortcomings, the social care mix in Ireland is a fascinating combination of the public, private and non-profit elements; it has evolved considerably in the last 5-10 years; and it gives endless food for thought regarding the original conundrum of the proper balance between the public and private spheres in the care of older persons. The task that now faces policy and decision makers will be equally, if not more, complex: defining and spelling out more clearly these boundaries between public and private responsibility and ensuring that regardless of the provider, the care delivered is of high quality and meets the needs of the older person. However, perhaps the most encouraging finding of this study concerns the dedication, hard work and genuine care that were evident from the interviews carried out with the home care workers themselves. They, alongside with the people they look after, must be the start and end points of any meaningful policy process, and ensuring good working conditions, on-going training and adequate remuneration for them is one of the best ways of guaranteeing that the aim of enabling older persons to remain living in their own homes can be achieved.

BIBLIOGRAPHY

Alber, J. (1995), "A framework for the comparative study of social services", *Journal of European Social Policy,* Vol. 5, No. 2, 131-149.

Boyle, G. (1997), "Community Care for Older People in Ireland: A Conceptual Critique of the Literature", *Administration,* Vol. 45, No. 2, 44-58.

Brady, J. (1994), National Council for the Elderly, "Proceedings of conference, Home Help Services for Elderly People In Ireland", Dublin, Royal Marine Hotel, Dun Laoghaire, 1st and 2nd of December, 1994.

Connell, P. and Pringle, D. (2004), *Population Ageing in Ireland. Projections 2002-2021,* Dublin: National Council on Ageing and Older People.

Convery, J. (2001), "Ireland", in: Blackman, T., Brodhurst, S. and Convery, J. (eds.), *Social Care and Social Exclusion: A Comparative Study of Older People's Care in Europe,* Basingstoke and New York: Palgrave.

Cullen, K., Delaney, S. and Duff, P. (2004), *Caring, Working and Public Policy,* Dublin: The Equality Authority.

Department of Health (2001), "Quality and Fairness: A Health System for You", Dublin: Stationery Office.

Department of Health Files 1937–1963, Department of Health, "Information on St. Brendan's After-Care Committee", by E. O'Brien, National Archives Reference Number L107/17.

Department of Health Files 1937–1963, Department of Health, "Outdoor Nursing Services (1951)", National Archives Reference Number L107/17.

Department of Health Files 1961, Department of Health, "Care of the Aged in their own Homes", A letter from the County Manager Galway County Council, 23 December 1961, National Archives Reference Number L119/1.

Department of Health Files 1961, Department of Health, "The Problem Presented by the Aged for the Hospital and Welfare Services", National Archives Reference Number L119/1.

Department of Social and Family Affairs (2002), "Study to Examine the Future Financing of Long-Term Care in Ireland", Dublin: Stationery Office.

Donoghue, F. (2001), "Volunteering in the Republic of Ireland: History, Socio-Economic Context and Meaning", Paper presented at Tipping the Balance Conference, UN International Year of Volunteering 2001, Ballyconnell, Co. Cavan, November 2001.

Donoghue, F., Anheiser, H.K. and Salamon, L.M. (1999), "Uncovering the Non-profit sector in Ireland, its economic value and significance", Dublin: The John Hopkins University Institute for Policy Studies and the National College of Ireland.

Dramin, A. (1983), "Home Help Services for the Elderly in the EHBA", *Administration* Vol. 34. No. 4, 527-534

Duffy, M.J. (2003), "The Voluntary Sector and The Personal Social Services", *Administration*, Vol. 51, Nos. 1–2, 173-190.

Finucane, P., Tieman, J. and Moane, G. (1993), "Support Services for Carers of Elderly People Living at Home", Dublin: National Council for the Elderly.

Garavan, R., Winder, R. and McGee, H. (2001), "Health and Social Services for Older People (HeSSOP): Consulting older people on health and social services: A survey of service use, experiences and needs", Dublin: National Council on Ageing and Older People.

Goodwin, F. (1997), National Council on Ageing and Older People, Conference proceedings, "Review of the Implementation of the Recommendations of the Years Ahead – A Policy for the Elderly and Implications for Future Policy on Older People in Ireland", Dublin, Jury's Hotel Ballsbridge, 11 and 12 September 1997.

Haase, T. and Pratschke, J. (2005), "Deprivation and its Spatial Articulation in the Republic of Ireland: New Measures of Deprivation based on the Census of Population, 1991, 1996 and 2002", NDP (National Development Plan), Area Development Management Limited, Dublin.

Haslett, D., Ruddle, H. and Hennessy, G. (1998), "The Future Organisation of the Home Help Service in Ireland", Dublin: NCAOP.

Health Act 1947, Irish Statute Book, available at http://www.irishstatutebook.ie/ZZA28Y1947.html

Health Act 1953, Irish Statute Book, available at http://www.irishstatutebook.ie /ZZA26Y1953.html

Health Act 1970, Irish Statute Book, available at http://www.irishstatutebook.ie/ ZZA1Y1970.html

Higginbotham, P. (2003), "The Workhouse in Ireland", available at http://users. ox.ac.uk/~peter/workhouse/.

Hughes, G., Williams, J., and Blackwell, S. (2004), "Demand and Cost of Long-Term Care Services, Country Report: Ireland", Dublin: Economic and Social Research Institute.

Hughes, G., Williams, J. and Blackwell, S. (2005), " Demand and cost of long-term care services, Country report: Ireland", GALCA project publication, Dublin : Economic and Social Research Institute.

Inter-Departmental Committee on the Care of the Aged (1968), "The Care of the Aged", Dublin: Stationery Office.

Inter-Departmental Committee on the Care of the Aged (1980), "Addendum to the *Care of the Aged"*, Report No 14/1980, Dublin: Eastern Health Board.

Lündström, F. and McKeown, K. (1994), "Home Help Service for Elderly People in Ireland", Dublin: National Council for the Elderly.

Mathew, D. (2002), "Independent Sector Home Care Provision in Northern Ireland", Belfast: Northern Ireland Social Care Council.

McGee, H.M., O'Hanlon, A., Barker, M., Stout, R., O'Neill, D., Conory, R., Hickey, A., Shelley. E. and Layte, R. (2005), *One Island – Two Systems: A Comparison of Health Status and Health and Social Service Use by Community-dwelling Older People in the Republic of Ireland and Northern Ireland,* Dublin: Institute of Public Health in Ireland.

Motel-Klingebiel, A., Tesch-Roemer, C. and von Kondratowitz, H. (2005), "Welfare states do not crowd out the family: Evidence for mixed responsibility from comparative analyses", *Ageing and Society,* Vol. 25, No. 6, 863-82.

Munday, B. (1996), "Conclusion: The Future for Social Care in Europe", in Munday, B. and Ely, P. (eds.), *Social Care in Europe,* London: Prentice Hall/Harvester Wheatsheaf, pp. 226-230.

National Economic and Social Forum (NESF) (2005), "Care for Older People*",* *NESF Report No. 32,* Dublin: NESF.

O'Dell, E. (ed) (2006), *Older People in Modern Ireland: Essays on Law and Policy,* Dublin: FirstLaw.

OECD (2005), *Long-term Care for Older People,* Paris: OECD.

O'Hanlon, A., McGee, H., Barker, M., Garavan, R., Hickey, A., Conroy, R. and O'Neill, D. (2005), *Health and Social Services for Older People II (HeSSOP II): Changing Profiles from 2000 to 2004,* Dublin: National Council on Ageing and Older People.

O'Loughlin, A. (2005), "Social Policy and Older People" in Quin, S., Kennedy, P., Matthews, A. and Kiely, G. (eds.), *Contemporary Irish Social Policy,* Dublin: UCD Press.

Pierce, M. (2006), "Social Care and Social Change in the Irish Welfare Economy", in Fanning, B. and M. Rush (eds.), *Irish Social Policy in Focus,* Dublin: UCD Press (publication forthcoming).

Pope Leo XIII (1891), "Encyclical Letter Rerum Novarum (On the Condition of Workers)".

Pope Pius XI (1931), *The Encyclical Quadragesimo Anno. The Social Order: Its Reconstruction and Perfection,* London: Catholic Truth Society.

Rostgaard, T. (2004), "The construction of consumerism – Free choice of care for the elderly in Denmark", paper presented at the Symposium "Consumerism of care for the elderly", at the Danish National Institute of Social Research (SFI), Copenhagen, 30 August 2004.

Ruddle, H., Donoghue, F. and Mulvihill, R. (1997), "The *Years Ahead* Report: A review of the implementation its recommendations", Dublin: National Council on Ageing and Older People.

Sipila, J., Anttonen, A. and Baldock, J. (2003), *The Young, the Old and the State*, Cheltenham, UK: Edward Elgar.

Society of St Vincent de Paul (1942), *Social Workers' Handbook. For the use of Catholic Social Workers in Dublin,* Dublin: Society of St Vincent de Paul.

The Commission on Nursing (1988), "A blueprint for the future" Dublin: Government of Ireland.

The Irish Catholic Registry and Almanac for 1954, Dublin: James Duffy and Co.

Timonen, V. (2004), "Evaluation of Homecare Grant Schemes in the NAHB and ECAHB", Dublin: Eastern Regional Health Authority.

Timonen, V. (2005), "Policy Paradigms and Long-Term Care: Convergence or Continuing Differences?", in Taylor-Gooby, P. (ed.), *Ideas and Welfare State Reform in Western Europe*, Basingstoke: Palgrave Macmillan.

Timonen, V. (2006), "Responsibility for the Costs of Long-Term Institutional Care: A Comparative Perspective", in O'Dell, E. (ed.), *Older People in Modern Ireland: Essays on Law and Policy,* Dublin: FirstLaw.

Timonen, V., Convery, J. and Cahill, S. (2006), "Care revolutions in the making? A comparison of cash-for-care programmes in four European countries", *Ageing & Society*, Vol. 26, 455-474.

Timonen, V. and McMenamin, I. (2002), "Future of Care Services in Ireland: Old Answers to New Challenges?", *Social Policy and Administration,* Vol. 36, No. 1, 20-35.

Working Party on Services for the Elderly (1988), "The Years Ahead – A Policy for the Elderly", Dublin: Government Publications.

Yeates, N. (1997), "Gender, Informal Care and Social Welfare: The Case of the Carer's Allowance", *Administration,* Vol. 45 No. 2, 21-43.